Well done, my dear frie... occasion this is. You have compiled your truth into print for all this world to see. What you saw, what you heard, what you experienced, and the proof that you have attained since Pearl's death is now organized in a complete package. Law enforcement, emergency teams, and government officials have tried to roadblock you from the beginning. But you FOUND the truth, in spite of their attacks, lies, and cover-ups. <u>GOD</u> knows what happened. And He led <u>YOU</u> to find your way to what really happened. It makes no difference who believes you and who does not. The truth is reality, and reality is what you witnessed. Anyone who chooses to turn away from reality, does so because they cannot, or will not, face that reality. But, their rejection of reality does not change the truth of what happened. And it doesn't change the reality of all that you experienced. Be at peace with your truth, regardless of what anyone may or may not believe, because it doesn't matter . . . God believes you . . . and I believe you . . . and many others do, too. And you know what? PEARL KNEW THE TRUTH. She would never have wanted you to feel any blame for what happened. She KNEW who murdered her, and she would be proud of what you went through to find out the truth and how hard you tried to get authority figures to listen. She would be proud of how far you have come and where you are today . . . and she would want peace for you after all the turmoil you have been through. She would understand everything you felt and endured.

You did a fantastic job in your writing. I'm so proud of you and my mother would be so proud, too!! You have been waiting for so many years for the day when you could scream out what you know, and this is it! God Bless you, Jeanie! Love you bunches!

—BETA READER, MINDY

Murdered *by* Mistake

Murdered
by Mistake

My Quest *for* Justice

Jeanie Hall

Jill Houston

CLEAN
WATER
LAND &
LEGACY
AMENDMENT

This activity is made possible, in part, by the voters of Minnesota, through a grant from the Five Wings Arts Council, thanks to a legislative appropriation from the Arts and Cultural Heritage Fund.

I dedicate this book to my twin sister,
who believed and supported me through the years.

Contents

Chapter 1   December 22, 1993 1

Chapter 2   My Beginnings. 9

Chapter 3   Marriage. Death. Birth. 12

Chapter 4   Smooth Criminal 16

Chapter 5   The Paper Trail. And Lack Thereof 25

Chapter 6   Men, Lies, and Money 29

Chapter 7   Jesus Take the Wheel 40

Chapter 8   The Hunter or the Hunted 48

Chapter 9   The Thread that Bound us Together. 52

Chapter 10 Remembering 54

Chapter 11 No Justice for Pearl 62

Chapter 12 Attorneys Sold My Property 70

Chapter 13 Homeless 77

Chapter 14 The Coroner's Inquest of 2001 79

Chapter 15 I Bought a Farm. 85

Chapter 16 My Four-Legged Children. 87

Chapter 17 One Last Call and My Darkest Days 91

Chapter 18 And the Murder Investigation Continues 95

Chapter 19 The Healer and the Healing. 101

Chapter 20 I'm Doing Better Now. 104

The longer I live, the more I realize the impact of attitude on my life. It is more important than the past, than education, than money, than circumstances, than failures, than success, than what people think, say, or do. It is more important than appearance, giftedness, or skill. The remarkable thing is--we have a choice every day of our lives regarding the attitudes we embrace for that day. We cannot change our past. We cannot change the inevitable. The only thing we can do is play the one string we have, and that is our attitude. I am convinced that life is ten percent what happens to me and ninety percent how I react to it. And so, it is with you. We are in charge of our attitudes.

—CHARLES SWINDOLL

Preface

My neighbor, Pearl, was murdered fifteen minutes after midnight on December 22, 1993.

I was there.

I saw the men who committed the act. I clearly saw their faces.

I heard their voices.

I knew that she was murdered.

After that night, I suffered traumatic amnesia, but five months later my memory began to come back. I was crazy with fear when I finally went to the police. But they had already closed the case. They did not believe me when I told them she was murdered. I told them, "They came for my attorney's records," and they did not believe me. The records reveal the illegal activities of several attorneys. The illegal transactions were started in 1983 and were continued by the divorce attorneys. My tumultuous divorce was obtained by arbitration to keep me out of the courtroom. All the records were pulled from the courthouse and were supposedly destroyed.

But they were not.

Instead, they were mistakenly given to me by my attorney's secretary.

I spent years collecting the data, records, and documentation that can be found in the back of this book. There are police and fire marshal reports, investigation reports from officials who were on the scene, an inquest done in 2001, letter between the attorneys on both sides, and letters sent to me by the county attorney.

All of the pieces to the case are needed for one to understand the sequence of events that led to the murder of Pearl. I have spent 28 years trying to get justice for her and convince the authorities that a heinous act took place that night.

There were two victims that night: one lived and one died.

Names and identifying details of certain individuals and places have been changed for privacy and safety reasons. The story you are about to read is a truthful recollection of actual events in my life.

Chapter 1

December 22, 1993

THE WEEK LEADING UP TO THAT FATEFUL night started like any other. On December 21, 1993, I had worked a day shift at the small local clinic in North Town. Nursing was my passion, and I was proud of my previous 30-year stint in Rochester, Minnesota working as a head nurse, clinical coordinator, supervisor, and emergency room nurse.

In this rural community, the closest hospital was 30 miles south of my home. On the evening of the 21st, that hospital had called to say they were extremely shorthanded and were desperate for help. They begged me to come and work the evening shift. I said "yes" even though I had just finished a full shift at the local clinic, and it was a 30+ mile drive one way.

They needed the help, and I needed the money. It was as simple as that.

I had always been a confident and competent nurse who was often called in to work on holidays. It wasn't unusual for me to work extra shifts after my regular shift at the clinic or even on my days off. Serving people and helping them heal was something that made me feel whole and it was something I loved to do. I had already given in to the fact that this was going to be a late night and my horses likely wouldn't get fed until around midnight.

That evening it was a bitterly cold, 25° below zero, and I was thankful my truck started after my evening shift ended. I left the hospital at 11:20 PM and pulled into my driveway around midnight. My horses would be hungry and eager to see me.

As always, I glanced at my neighbors' homes as I drove by partially out of curiosity, but also just to be a good neighbor. We all looked out for each other in our little corner of the world. George was an elderly man who lived all alone, and his driveway was just a few turns before mine. Pearl was my next-door neighbor, and I always made a point to visually check on her house as I drove by. She was in her late 80's, lived alone, didn't drive or own a car, and had trouble moving around because of her arthritic knees.

As I made the slow drive past Pearl's house, I saw that the house was completely dark except for an odd flicker of light in the kitchen window. The flicker made me pause for a moment because I knew that Pearl would have been sound asleep at this late hour. It was unusual to see any sort of movement.

I also found it odd that there was an unfamiliar car parked behind her pine tree in such a haphazard way that the branches of the tree were actually touching the glass of the windshield. Through the darkness, I could see the distinctive round headlights of the car, which looked to be white in color. I knew her granddaughter had a similar car, but the way it was wedged up under the low-hanging branches was unusual, to say the least.

Bone-tired and ready for my bed, I dismissed the strange car as a holiday guest since Christmas Eve was only a few days away. I climbed out of my truck, anxious to check on my horses. As tired as I was, I did notice what a gorgeous northern evening it was. Despite the freezing temps, the sky was clear, and the stars were so bright that I felt like I could see for miles. Thanks to the nighttime glow, I didn't even bother grabbing a flashlight to illuminate my path.

Bundled up in my warmest winter clothing, I hurried around the barn, pouring grain in a bucket, and made my way to my 100-foot pole shed. I noticed my two young stallions were not waiting for me outside the door as usual. Instead, they were across the pen, huddled up close to a fence that was directly behind Pearl's house. Their actions and demeanor told me that they were very nervous and agitated about something. Their eyes were fixed on the backside of Pearl's house.

Historically, horses have always been prey animals, so they have a deeply ingrained sense of fight or flight in their DNA. They are like watchdogs and, if you pay attention, they will always tell you when something is not right. That night, it was obvious to me that my horses were frightened and uneasy. They kept snorting in fear and their tails were arched in alarm. Instead of welcoming me home and wanting food, they began to pace back and forth with their full attention on something at Pearl's house. Something had spooked them, and they were trying to tell me that they smelled danger. Something was not right, and I decided to walk the fence line to see what it was.

What I saw next chilled me to the bone.

When I reached the fence behind Pearl's house, the lights were now on, and I could hear angry voices. This was not normal behavior since Pearl was not a confrontational person. I could hear men's voices and it was apparent that a heated argument was taking place. I could hear Pearl's raised voice as well, but I could not make out the words. Then, a very short man suddenly appeared on her back deck. The deck faced the southwest corner of the house, so I could see the stranger clearly even though he could not see me. He paced back and forth while lighting a cigarette. Every few steps, he would pause as if he were straining to hear what the angry voices inside Pearl's house were saying.

He had no idea I was there, and I wasn't about to let him know that I was. A much taller man suddenly dashed out of the house, and his exit was immediately followed by a bright, explosion-like flash from inside the house. The sound was jarring and sounded like the crack of someone slamming a screen door with all their strength. The brief flash of fire lit up the night sky. By the light of the burning blaze, I could see the men's faces clearly.

And I will never forget those faces as long as I live. I recognized the shorter of the two men as my ex-husband's partner from our car wash. The taller man was vaguely familiar and even slightly resembled a relative of my ex-husband.

Both men left the deck quickly and went to stand by the west side of Pearl's house. The crisp, cold, and calm evening air allowed their panicked voices to carry across the pen to where I was hiding and watching.

"This isn't Jeanie's house!" the first man snarled to the other. "You didn't have to do that. She was only an old woman!"

The taller man slapped both hands onto the shoulders of the shorter man and gave him a violent shake. "I had to do it because she could identify me."

My mind was racing and spinning. I couldn't catch my breath and my legs felt like rubber. I wanted to race into the now-smoldering kitchen, but I didn't dare reveal myself to the men. As much as I wanted to pretend that she was instead trapped in her bedroom and needing my help, I knew in my heart that it was too late for Pearl. Her life had been extinguished. All I could do was pray that she was already dead before fire consumed her.

Terror washed over me as I began to realize that I was also in danger. These men had gone to the wrong house and now that they realized it, they would either run or come one driveway over and finish their original mission. I needed to get into the safety of my house without being seen by the men. I did not know in those moments that my life was about to change forever. I just knew I needed to focus on saving my own life. I knew I could not let these men see me.

To this day, I cannot remember how I made it back to the gate on my property and to where my horses now were. I remember hiding behind my horse, Chip, in an effort to keep him between myself and the horror that had just happened at my neighbor's house. I remember the two men and the darkness. I remember the terrifying moments when I didn't know where they were or if they had seen me flee.

The fire and chaos had dissipated, and everything was now dark and deathly still. Then I heard the muffled thuds of car doors shutting. Car headlights suddenly lit up the darkness and I could see the mysterious white car backing out from behind the tree and driving down the driveway to the main road. I took the chance that the two intruders wouldn't look out the back window as they drove off and I bolted for the safety of my house. I ran down through the pole shed, turned off the lights, and peered towards my house. If the men had turned north, they would have come by my driveway and would have recognized my truck and known where I lived. If they turned south, I would be out of their line of vision . . . **and safe.**

Thankfully, their car turned south and drove away from me. Shaken and sickened, the static in my traumatized mind could only think of one thing; **get to my house.** I slowly walked toward my home, as quietly as I could, and used the cover of night to my advantage. My nerves were on edge and every little sound in the night made me jump. My mind was spinning, and I couldn't seem to get a handle on what I had just witnessed.

As I stumbled to the safety of my home, I stopped and glanced over at Pearl's house. Everything was once again quiet and still. Did I imagine it all? The main thought racing through my mind was, "Something bad happened there. Something bad enough to make me very afraid."

What happened after those moments was a dark, blank hole in my memory for many, many months. The next thing I remembered was standing at my bedside, staring at my alarm clock, and wondering how it could be 1:00 AM already. Typically, my nightly chores took 30 minutes. There were 30 minutes that I could not account for.

My brain and body felt like lead, as if I had just run 100 miles and my body just couldn't take another step. My brain felt thick and muddy, as if I were locked in a dream that I couldn't wake up from and my eyes were filled with tears. My house and the outside world were eerily quiet. I remember thinking, "Did I just dream it all?"

It took every ounce of my strength to make it under the covers that night. I recall nothing more until the next morning. I was awakened by someone pounding on my door. By the time I got out of bed and dressed, I could see a Schwan's delivery man walking hastily away from my door and back to his vehicle. Seconds later, he roared out of my driveway and down the road. I was still having trouble thinking clearly and I was still feeling depleted and exhausted.

Then the phone rang. It was my cousin calling to tell me that there was chatter on the CB radio that there had been a fire at Pearl's the night before. Knowing I was a nurse, she kept urging me to go next door to see if I could help. I just couldn't. Through my kitchen window, I could see the ambulance pulling down Pearl's driveway and then the anxiety hit me like a lead weight.

A short time later, my cousin called me back and her first words were, "Pearl is dead!" I started to sob uncontrollably.

"It was supposed to be me!"

I placed a long-distance call to my sister and those were the first words I remember blurting out. I was rambling and hysterical and she was thoroughly confused and skeptical. In frustration, I called two other friends and told them the same thing.

"It was supposed to be me!"

But no one seemed to understand. My memory was sketchy, and I couldn't make the words come out of my mouth. But I knew I was scared. Very scared. My mind was in a fog and my nursing experience clued me in to the fact that I was likely in shock. Needing to take care of my animals and hoping that the fresh air would clear my muddled mind, I went outside. I tried to keep my eyes away from Pearl's house because, honestly, I was not mentally, physically, or emotionally prepared for what I might see. Like a robot, I went through the motions of caring for my animals and then getting ready for work at the clinic at noon.

My friends at work could tell something was wrong because I was simply not acting like myself. The secretary at the front desk asked me, "What is wrong with you?" My eyes overflowed with tears as I told her, "I can't tell you". The next day, I drove to Pearl's son and daughter-in-law's business with the sole purpose of asking them how she had died. Their response was, "She was baking when she had a heart attack, fell, and accidentally caught herself on fire."

I remember feeling a sense of profound relief. I felt relieved that I would no longer have to try to make sense of memories that didn't want to be retrieved. Being told her death was an accident felt like a ton of bricks had been lifted off me. I went on with my life with no further memory of that fateful night.

It took me over five months to remember the horrible details of that night. It's only been recently, during the writing of this book, that I discovered a medical diagnosis called traumatic amnesia. I firmly believe this is what came over me in 1993. It was my brain's way of coping with something that was simply too horrible to fathom.

There was one detail that I knew to be 100 percent accurate, that evening was a clear case of mistaken identity. It was a case of two men who had harm and destruction on their minds. I believe these men were told to break into my home and retrieve the damning divorce attorneys' records that I had been lucky enough to get in error. Looking back on the day those records entered my life, I knew my initial gut instincts had been right; someone would come for those records and take them back any way they could.

And sadly, it was Pearl who paid the price for their error.

I also know that these men, men who I knew from the car wash business, were familiar with my life and schedule. They knew that I had a habit of picking up evening or night shifts around the holidays and that those shifts were at hospitals far from my home. They knew they had a window of opportunity to ransack my house that night to retrieve what they were instructed to find before I got home.

I was filled with overwhelming guilt at the realization that the men went one driveway too far, and that someone I cared about died instead of me.

Chapter 2

My Beginnings

IT WAS AN EARLY SPRING DAY IN MARCH 1941 when I made my arrival into this world as one of two tiny girls. My twin sister, Mary, and I joined my older brother, Robert, who was two and a half years older than us. I was born with hazel eyes and dark hair and my twin sister was blonde with blue eyes. We may have looked different from each other, but we were as close as twins can be.

When I was about six years old, I woke up during the night, looked out of my bedroom window, and noticed the sky was bright orange in color. My sleepy brain didn't identify it as the glow from a large fire and it wasn't until the next morning that I found out that my father's auto dealership had burned to the ground. He had very little insurance, so this was a horrible loss to our family. But my father did not give up. He built a new building on the old property and continued with his dealership.

When Mary and I were nine years old, we both became very sick and ended up in a hospital in the Twin Cities. A spinal tap was performed on both of us, and we were both diagnosed with polio. I was placed in an oxygen tent and was unconscious for three days with a high fever. There was an iron lung always running beside my bed in case I needed to be put inside to save my life. Luckily, my fever broke, and I spent many months in physical therapy to regain my strength. To this day, I am weak on my left side from my head to my toes.

When I was 13 and about to be confirmed and baptized at the church, my father visited the hospital in the big city for a series of tests. Instead of being sent home, he was admitted. Our family piled into the car and my mom frantically made the drive to see him, only to be told when we arrived that he was dying. He had been given a new drug for his diabetes and the drug reacted negatively to his system. Within hours, he was in complete renal shut-down; he died that night. I still remember being angry at him for dying for weeks and months after his death. How could he leave us like that? He was my big, strong daddy who was supposed to live and take care of us forever.

It was at that time that I believed I lost my childhood. By necessity, Mary and I were forced into the role of caregivers for my mother, who was fragile in both health and emotion. We cooked for her, cleaned, fetched her what she needed, and tried very hard never to do anything to upset her. We needed to grow up fast. I also remember never being resentful about my new role within my family. I just did what needed to be done. I loved my mother and was committed to helping her navigate life the best way she could.

Even though she was sick and fragile, my mother continued to manage my dad's auto dealership. We did not have a lot of money, but we did not ask for much. As we got older, Mary and I both got summer jobs in town or at local resorts. It was during this time that I stumbled upon my passion for nursing. It started when I accepted a job at a newly opened nursing home in my hometown. I loved the work and it brought me great joy to do something special for my patients. I loved that work so much that, after I graduated from high school, I decided to go to college in Rochester, Minnesota to study nursing.

The Methodist-Kahler School of Nursing I attended was affiliated with the world-famous Mayo Clinic, and that fact made me swell with pride. I also knew my mother could barely afford to send me to this school, but she insisted. She told me that she was proud of me and wanted me to do well. Those words of encouragement meant the world to me.

After graduation, I dove headfirst into my chosen career. I loved every minute of it. In the beginning, I worked as a staff nurse during the night shift and cared for as many as 21 patients at times. Every morning after my shift, I had to report everything to the head nurse, who was a former army nurse with a reputation for being tough. But she was highly respected and was very experienced. She told me that I impressed her, something that I knew was not easy to do. I kept doing my very best work for this mentor and eventually, I became the head nurse of the Gynecology Unit in that hospital.

I felt like I was on top of the world.

But that high moment in my life would not last. I was soon caught up in an orchestrated series of events that summed up a lifelong struggle to survive.

The following chapters will reveal all the pieces of the puzzle that need to be in place before you, the reader, will understand all the events that lead to the murder of my neighbor: a heinous act that was meant for me.

As I look back on my 80 years on this planet, I can see the pattern of chaos, abuse, and deceit at the hands of a variety of men, men who thought nothing of having no conscience or sense of decency and were perfectly happy living a life filled with greed, lies, and cruelty.

These men ranged from common criminals to successful professionals who were deeply involved in white-collar crimes. They included men who were once my trusted companions and even business partners. The common thread they all shared was a desire to line their own pockets while leading me toward financial ruin.

And they all would have preferred that I simply disappear.

Chapter 3

Marriage. Death. Birth.

I BELIEVE THAT BECAUSE OF MY STRUGGLES in my childhood years, and the need to be obedient and subservient at home, my entire personality had shifted by the time I reached adulthood. I had morphed into an obedient homebody. That learned habit may have been the result of having to bite my tongue, stifle my feelings, and take the "high road" on things to avoid upsetting my grieving and ailing mother. But whatever the reason, that unhealthy personality trait followed me into adulthood.

Not long after my promotion to head nurse, I met my first husband Vernon. He had recently lost his father and, since I knew what that felt like, I offered advice and kind words. Looking back now, I don't know why I married Vernon. He ended up being more of a child than a husband to me. He was needy and dependent to the point where I felt smothered by him most of the time. As my frustration grew, and his dependency on me became toxic and stifling, our love eroded, and we grew apart. Despite everything, I couldn't seem to find the strength to leave him, even though I knew it was best for both of us.

During this trying time in my life, my mother's health took a turn for the worse. I wonder now whether, back then, she just couldn't find the strength to go on without her husband any longer. Her life had not been easy, due to her poor health, but she had worked hard to raise three good kids. I also believe that, with all three of us married and on our own, she felt her work was done and it was her time to go. We lost her in the summer of 1965 when a fluid buildup in her chest caused a fatal heart attack. Mary, Robert, and I were devastated.

Despite being in an unhappy marriage, a few years after my mother's passing, I became a mom as well. My first child was a son named, William, and we welcomed him into the world in 1967. He was a beautiful baby and how I wished my mother had been there to see him! William was "preemie-sized" even though he was full-term and only weighed three pounds and six ounces at birth. The doctors kept him in the hospital until he tipped the scales at five pounds, which took about a month.

My little boy had a rough start to life and his birth was complicated. His father was too intimidated to take care of him. True to form, my overly helpless husband never changed a diaper or fed his baby. Luckily, I was able to hire a babysitter who wasn't unnerved by William's small size and fragility. It allowed me to go back to work and continue to support our growing family.

I continued to be the head nurse at the hospital and was able to transition into working day shifts, which better suited being a new mom. I made a good salary at that time, and thanks to my income, we were able to buy a three-bedroom rambler in town. Not long after we bought our new home, I found out I was pregnant again. Nine months later, I gave birth to a beautiful baby girl that we named Sherry.

Sherry was also preemie-sized like her brother despite being a full-term baby. She too weighed only three pounds and six ounces at birth and followed in her older brother's footsteps of needing to remain in the hospital until she gained weight. Needless to say, my life was blessed, but it was also getting more complicated.

Once again, I located a babysitter who was comfortable watching two fragile babies, and this allowed me to take the time I needed to enjoy the two things that were keeping me sane: my job and my horses. Whenever a sliver of free time would present itself in my hectic days, I would take riding lessons at the stable where I boarded my horses. The stable owner was a wonderful woman who let me board my horses there for free if she could use them to give students lessons.

My marriage had not improved at all. In fact, it had deteriorated even more. I immersed myself in being the best mom, nurse, and horse owner that I could be, but I couldn't deny that my relationship with my husband was on a downward spiral.

As the weeks turned into months, Vernon's self-absorbed ways worsened, and he would often forget our anniversary and the family's birthdays.

One year, when he forgot our anniversary once again, he threw a piece of paper on the table and snarled, "There. The goddamn horse is yours." The horse he was referring to was one that was stabled at the same facility where I kept my own horse. He was an abused and terrified gelding named Command. He was only two years old and was not yet broken to ride. He mistrusted men and was labeled a "problem horse." Despite his issues, I had been drawn to him. Once he became mine, I worked with him constantly. I earned his trust and we bonded. I knew that if he was ever sold to anyone else, he was destined for the kill barn because he was so unmanageable for everyone but me and my kids. That wasn't going to happen on my watch.

After lots of hard work, patience, and persistence, I finally broke him to be rideable. Over the many years we were together, Command never gave me any problems. He gave me 200 percent in everything he did, and he ultimately became a champion endurance horse.

The wonderful gift of Command did not change the fact that Vernon was a terrible husband. He was also not faithful to me and his dalliances with other women got worse when he took an on-the-road sales job. It became commonplace for him to announce he was going out of state for two weeks, but he refused to tell me where he was going. To this day, I suspected he had several different girlfriends on his sales route.

Finally, I had enough and told him one day, "I want you gone." Furious, but not really believing me, he started to pack items he seldom used from the top shelf of the closet. I knew he was waiting for me to change my mind, but I held strong. I was not afraid of being a single mother and I felt like I had been raising my children alone for ten years anyway.

I filed for divorce from Vernon, and he was served his papers on his birthday in 1974. The kids adjusted well since their dad was not involved in their lives that much. At the time William was in second grade and during class he stood up, interrupted the teacher, and announced to the class very proudly, "*Me, my mom, and my sister . . . We divorced my dad.*" When the teacher told me this, she noted that he said it confidently and without anger or blame in his voice.

I knew I had made the right decision.

Chapter 4

Smooth Criminal

IT TOOK MY HEART SOME TIME TO HEAL from the disappointment of my failed marriage. But over a year later, when I went to a car wash, I met a delightful man named Ed who was the manager of the facility. We chatted while my car was being washed and I realized that I had met him at a party years before. As we talked, Ed revealed that he also was divorced and had two sons that lived with their mother. He was around my age, was tall, dark, and handsome, and we had the common experience of divorce and co-parenting. Our paths crossed numerous times and he asked me out on a date not long after our encounter at the car wash.

When Ed asked me out for the first time, it was just before deer hunting opener weekend. I turned him down because I already had plans to go North and do some deer hunting with friends and family. I loved deer hunting and always saved up my work vacation so I could hunt on opening weekend. For our group, it was a weekend that we looked forward to all year long.

My brother owned a hunting shack deep in the woods that could sleep ten to twelve people, so there were always plenty of folks to laugh, chat, and hunt with. On the wall of the cabin was a handmade tally board of sorts. Every time someone harvested a deer, they would write the date, the location, and the sex of the deer on the wall. It was like a perpetual timeline of past hunts. Some of my favorite moments of deer camp involved hearing all the deer hunting stories from the years gone by. Most I had already heard a handful of times, but I didn't care. It was all part of the deer camp experience.

As I look back now, I wish had just said NO to that first date inquiry from Ed. I wish I had just walked away and kept him as a friend. I think another thing that attracted me to Ed was the fact that he was so different from my first husband. He was hard-working, confident, and seemingly level-headed. He was an independent man with a strong personality, and I was drawn to that. However, at the time I did *not* know that Ed was an alcoholic: that would have been a deal-breaker, had I known in the beginning. But he kept that character flaw secret from many others, including me.

As I got to know Ed, I learned that he had grown up on a farm in southern Minnesota. He was one of three children and the only boy. His parents were farmers who never stopped struggling financially. He shared with me that Christmas in his childhood home was always bleak and joyless. One Christmas, he recalled getting only a roll of Lifesavers in his Christmas Stocking.

As a child, Ed would get terrible ear infections, but his parents didn't have the money to take him to a doctor. Because he was forced to endure years of suffering through the pain of these infections, he had significant hearing loss and eventually lost his hearing altogether.

Despite being clinically deaf, Ed attended school without knowing sign language or having any sort of learning assistance. It wasn't until his adult years that he was able to afford hearing aids. Though Ed's mother was quiet and pleasant, she lived under the silent abuse of a controlling husband. He was very much like a dictator when it came to parenting and always demanded meals be served at a specific time--no exceptions. I'll never forget the first time I met Ed's father when we were dating. His first words to me were not, "Hello" or "Nice to meet you." Instead, he asked, "Are you Democrat or Republican?" I replied that I was neutral and favored neither. Ed's father smirked at his son and said to me, "You surely got through that one right."

In the beginning, Ed appeared to be a good, kind, and successful man. But as the years progressed, that veneer began to slip away to reveal a side of him that was much more disturbing to me. It was a side that exposed his narcissism and sociopathic tendencies. Throughout the marriage, the red flags were there. But I just chose to avert my eyes in embarrassment, and even a little bit of fear. His talent for expertly lying and covering up his actions, paired with my naïveté, was a recipe for a toxic relationship.

In December 1976, Ed surprised me with an engagement ring. I was thrilled and began making wedding plans. That same day, Ed also told me he had an opportunity to purchase the car wash that he managed. He asked if I would support him if he chose to go ahead with the purchase. At the time, I had no debt, my car was paid for, and I had money in the bank, so the idea of possibly helping my future husband grow the business was exciting.

Again, I should have said *no.*

Early in 1977, I sold my house and with my own money, bought my farm. However, Ed told the owner of the car wash that *he*, in fact, had paid for my farm and it was a gift *to me*. He even took the seller out to my new property and bragged that he had bought it as a token of his love for me. The seller believed him completely.

The day I was introduced to the seller, he made a point to mention how impressed he was that Ed had bought a farm for me. Shocked and mortified, I looked at Ed, who responded by subtly shaking his head and putting his finger to his lips as a "don't tell" signal. Ed later told me that he had made up that lie because the seller had revealed that he didn't feel that Ed was a serious buyer because he wasn't married.

The old me wanted to shout and rave at my husband-to-be. But the quiet, meek, subservient me simply shrugged it off and went along with it.

That's a decision I now regret.

Despite all my concerns and the uneasy feelings that nagged at my intuition day and night, we were married in June of 1977. After our wedding, Ed moved into my house, and I continued to pay the bills. We honeymooned at Lake of the Woods in Northern Minnesota, but it wasn't exactly a honeymoon because my new husband's parents, his sister and her husband, and our kids (his two and my two) all came along. We spent the week fishing and ate fish for supper and lunch every day. Those were the good times at the lake.

After we were married, Ed's parents came for a visit and stayed a couple of weeks. My husband was not very fond of his parents. He basically just tolerated their presence. One day while I was visiting with his mother, she turned to me and said, "You know Ed is not a good man, right?" I answered, "He is good for me."

He was "good for me" during our first two years of marriage, but that all soon fell apart and he proved to me over and over that his mother had been right all along. Even now it is hard to see how gullible and wrong I was about my second husband.

It wasn't long after our marriage, that we purchased the car wash in Rochester. I noticed my second husband's bad habits becoming even more pronounced. He was drinking more during the day, even though I didn't allow beer on my property. After work, he and his employees would stay at the car wash and get drunk together on beer. Ed would hide bottles of hard liquor on my farm, and I would catch him sneaking a nip from a bottle that had been hidden in a pile of hay, behind his vehicle seat, and even in our pole barn.

I told him I would not tolerate drinking and if he did not quit, I would get a divorce. He did refrain from drinking for quite a long time and there was a small level of peace in our marriage until around 1980.

In 1980, Ed purchased a grain elevator in southern Minnesota with the intention of building an ethanol plant on the same site. I didn't find out until years later that, on February 25, 1982, Ed took out an SBA loan for $340,000 at 18.5 percent. With that money, he built an ethanol plant. My husband rented a house next to the ethanol plant and spent six days a week in a town that was a couple hours from our home.

Even though things didn't feel right, I continued to support his new business just as I had done with his other ventures. I even worked a couple of days a week at the car wash as a cashier, and I would faithfully make trips to Ed's new house to bring him supplies when he needed things.

Since he was not present to run the car wash, Ed hired a new manager. This man, who I will call Roger, was made the assistant manager of the car wash. He made my skin crawl the moment I met him. Roger was also a distinctive-looking man; only five feet tall with a heavyset build. He was also a heavy drinker. Roger followed Ed's instructions like a trained monkey and did whatever was asked of him. It almost felt like a form of hero worship, and it was a little unsettling to watch.

The workers at the car wash were not exactly what one would consider "employee of the month" material. They were the type of folks I would categorize as the ones needing a second chance in life. They were felons, drug addicts, alcoholics, homeless, work-release county prisoners, and a few were visibly mentally ill. Working at the car wash was hardly a glamorous job and the pay was barely above minimum wage. It was the sort of employment opportunity that attracted the kind of worker who needed quick money with no desire for longevity.

Unfortunately, Ed's employees brought their bad habits and their criminal behaviors with them to work, but neither he nor Roger did anything to discourage them. There were rumors floating around town about stolen property and drug deals happening on the business' property. Again, I bit my lip, swallowed my suspicions, and buried myself in my work and horses.

It was during these trying times that I became even more interested in Endurance Riding with my horse, Command. An

Endurance Ride is a race consisting of a distance of 50 to 100 miles in one day. I felt that this new venture was something I needed just as much as my beloved gelding.

Command had a stocky build but had enough Arabian in him for me to consider competing with him in 50-mile endurance rides. This horse loved to run and had spirit and spunk like no other horse I'd ever owned. When I shared my new adventure with my vet, he told me that Command would never be able to be an endurance horse because he was a nervous horse. Command was also intimidated by men; a result of his being cruelly treated in his younger years.

After much planning and training, Command and I showed up for our first Endurance Ride event together. Vet checks are usually done during the ride to assess a horse's pulse rate and respiration. This was a cause for concern for me since these vet checks were usually done by men. I had a real fear that, because of his fear of men, my horse would not be able to pass his pulse and respiratory check and we would be eliminated from the race. But luck was with us on that day and the vet at our very first race was female. Command passed his checks with flying colors. We made it through the 50-mile ride with no issues and, from that moment on, we were both hooked! I was so proud of both of us. It was a much-needed bright spot in my tumultuous life.

During a time when I knew my marriage was failing and my husband was up to no good, getting involved in these competitions soothed my nerves and calmed my fears. My daughter also began competing with me and together we excelled. Sherry competed as a Junior Rider with Command in 1982 and together they became Midwest Champions. She was only 12 at the time and, ironically, Command was twelve years old as well.

My son William came with us when we participated in endurance rides. He was part of my "pit crew" and would carry gallons of water to the rest stops to cool my horse down prior to the vet check. He excelled at this job, and everybody wanted him to pit for them. On one of the rides, I came into the rest stop, and apparently,

I was giving too many orders. In response, my son picked up five gallons of water and poured it directly on me saying, "Now get off your horse, go over there, and rest."

The three of us spent every other weekend competing in competitive and endurance rides all over the Midwest. As I raced, I always recited this poem in my head. I am not entirely sure where this verse originated from, but it was a mantra to which I hold fast to even to this day. I've long forgotten where I first saw this verse and several searches on the Internet have come up with no source. What I do know is that this verse came to me when I needed it most.

Horses are God-like creatures.
Higher than all others,
formed by the sea,
wind and earth, but mightier than all of these.
Because with *the strength of the sea,*
the swiftness of the wind,
and the stability of the earth,
he makes his rider an Earth God.

Equine Endurance Ride events were held from April to November, and I feel as though I have seen the Midwest Region from the back of a horse! These were such happy times for me. These competitions were my therapy, and I would ride six days a week and often had three horses ready for competition. During this time, I also found a new passion for visiting sale barns, where I routinely bought horses that were sentenced to death and turned them into champions. That first summer of racing was a turning point for me in many ways; it was a year I will never forget.

There was one definite dark spot that summer of 1984, though. I had to take Ed to the hospital because he had fallen off a horse and broken his ankle. While we were at the hospital, the assistant manager of the car wash, Roger Hammer, walked into our room and was noticeably intoxicated.

The first words out of his mouth were, *"Jessica is dead."* Jessica was Roger's beautiful six-year-old daughter. When we asked what happened, Roger slurred that he had pulled into the toy-littered driveway and hit something. He also revealed to us in his alcohol-soaked words that he had wanted to "teach her a lesson," so he stepped on the accelerator so he deliberately could run over Jessica's toys as punishment. He didn't see his only child playing happily with those toys. She died instantly.

What struck me the most was that Roger didn't show any remorse and never shed a tear. It was a true indication of his personality, and I wish I had paid more attention to that telling detail. The funeral was held a week later, and it was one of the saddest funerals I've ever been to in my life.

After that horrific event, my marriage and private life began to take an even darker turn for the worst. There was unshakeable darkness that kept descending over me and I couldn't shake the feeling of dread in the pit of my stomach. My husband's bad behaviors and shady deals were beginning to leak out for the world to see and I was caught right in the middle.

One of the more mortifying revelations came from learning that Ed had become friendly with the young vice president of a local bank in southern Minnesota. This bank was in the same town as my husband's ethanol business.

The vice president of the bank had initially been excited to have a plant come to town because it encouraged growth, development, and potential employment in the small community. But Ed, with all his manipulative ways, talked the young, easily persuaded vice president into loaning him more money, unbeknownst to the bank president. This "under the desk" deal was all fine and dandy until the vice president received word that his bank was going to be audited. He panicked and demanded that Ed pay the loan back before the vice president was caught and fired for this wrongdoing.

As Ed retold this story to me, he was chuckling. He shared that, in light of this looming audit, he suggested to the vice president that he should just "burn down the bank" to cover up the illegal bank loan. Sadly, the frightened but honest man did indeed attempt to burn the bank down and destroy the records. The bank building did not burn, and the vice president was caught, charged with arson, and sent to jail for his actions. Ed was subpoenaed for the trial but told me that when asked about the debt he denied it. He told me he stated in court, "Are you going to believe me, or the man who attempted to burn down the bank?" Ed seemed to think it was funny, that he had manipulated a "gullible kid."

My husband's actions made me sick to my stomach. But again, I did nothing but keep my mouth shut, my head down, and stay in my subservient cocoon. In 1983, Ed walked away from his ethanol plant and returned to our home in Rochester. I obviously knew he had walked away from the ethanol plant, but I'd also been led to believe that the debts were all taken care of when the assets of that business were confiscated. It was a lie.

The sketchy business deals became more frequent, and I found myself agreeing to things that I never should have. When you are married, you trust that the person you love will not lead you astray. I trusted that Ed knew what was best for us and wouldn't get us involved in dangerous and questionable ventures.

I was wrong.

To get through our daily routine, I slipped into a mode that I can only describe as numb. The fiery woman that I once was, had given way to someone who was shy, afraid, subservient, and maybe even clueless.

The ramifications of being uninformed and manipulated by the man who had said a wedding vow to protect and honor me were about to overcome me like a speeding freight train.

And I was not ready.

Chapter 5

The Paper Trail.
And Lack Thereof

WHEN I LOOK BACK ON THE TRIGGERING factors that led to Pearl's murder, I can see clearly that madness began with one thing, **paper**.

Paper files, to be exact. Legal files crammed with damning evidence of wrongdoings of many men in positions of power. These were files that were supposed to be destroyed but were rescued by myself and my sister.

The years between 1986 and 1993 were filled with reams of paper in the form of legal briefs, arbitrations, depositions, interrogatories, divorce papers, court records, injunctions, lawsuits, and bills. A lot of bills. It was 60+ months of hell that left me broke and broken.

But the paper trail began even *before* I filed for divorce from my second husband. In 1983, Ed walked away from his ethanol plant in southern Minnesota, returned to our home in Rochester, and went back to work at the car wash. Now that he was home again, I accepted a position as Night Supervisor at a major Rochester community hospital. My income continued to pay our bills.

During this time, Ed and I continued to grow further and further apart. We barely spoke to one another, and he tried to avoid me whenever he could. This became more obvious when he developed the habit of coming home every night after the rest of us had already eaten, only to retire to the family room to watch TV. He never wanted to be disturbed and I would go to bed alone every night. We never said "hello" or "goodbye" or "good morning" or "good night." We were more like roommates than a married couple.

During this time, Ed also began hiding all of our assets. He assured me all debt from the failed ethanol business had been satisfied and we were "in the clear" financially. To do damage control on the loss of his ethanol business, he hired a law firm in Rochester to transfer all his personal assets out of his name and put them in my name and Roger Hammer's name.

Through a series of questionable deals and not-so-legal contracts, I became part owner of the car wash along with Roger, the man that I already despised. A new company, M&H Properties, was formed. This company also made Roger and me 50/50 shareholders. To facilitate this, the law firm had a corporate attorney draw up a lengthy and complex partnership agreement.

When presented with the completed document to sign, I regret that I did not take the time to read all of it before signing in the presence of an attorney. Later, when I did read it through, I discovered a clause at the end that did not sit well with me. The clause stated that, in the event of the death of one of the partners, the deceased party's 50 percent shares would be automatically transferred to the remaining partner. Meaning, if I passed away, Roger would get all of it. Or vice versa.

The thought that I was in business with a possible sociopath **did** cross my mind. It was not a pleasant thought.

Later, this same attorney also transferred our other properties into Roger's name, a move that I thought was highly suspect. When

I confronted Ed and asked if that move was even legal, I was told; "Of course it is! An attorney is drawing up the papers so, of course, it's all above board."

Once again, I ignored my intuition that something was wrong and let my trusting and naïve nature dictate my decisions. To add to the already unfolding madness, my marriage to Ed was on an irreversible downhill slide. He had begun drinking heavily again and was mentally and verbally abusive. I was miserable and embarrassed that my second marriage was failing just like my first. I felt sick and defeated all the time, but still I said nothing.

I now know that over the many years of dysfunction and trauma, I tended to resort to denial as a coping mechanism. I shut my brain off to any possibilities that bad things could happen and that there was danger looming in my future. My world felt like it was crashing around me and all I could do was paste a fake smile on my face and continue to put one foot in front of the next and hope the next day would be better. I wrapped myself in a cloak of numbness and continued to find grace and comfort in my kids, my work at the hospital, and my equine endurance competitions on the weekends. But even these things couldn't protect me from the storm that was brewing.

Soon a rumor began circulating around town that Ed was having an affair with a bar waitress named Rosa. When I heard, I knew this was the last straw. I had had enough. My relationship with my daughter had completely broken down as well, thanks to the underhanded bad-mouthing that Ed was doing behind my back. He even bought my daughter a car, without my approval, so she could have freedom to go whenever she wanted. My veneer of "everything is fine" cracked and I collapsed onto the grass in my front yard, crying in despair. I wanted to run away from everything, but my horses kept me from leaving. They needed me and I needed them.

In the fall of 1986, I finally told Ed I wanted a divorce.

His reaction started out as *"I don't blame you,"* but quickly morphed into *"You will pay for this!"* as he stormed from the house with his clothes in his arms. Deep down in the pit of my stomach, I knew this was a defining moment and that life would be even more difficult going forward. To add salt to the wound, I found out that it took less than a week for Ed to shack up with his bar waitress girlfriend in a fourplex we both owned across town.

Knowing I was in for a hell of a fight, I began looking for an attorney in town who could help me with my divorce. I knew this process was going to be complicated and difficult and I needed a lawyer who could handle the case and put up with Ed's lies and deception.

The first attorney I met with did not meet my expectations. Then I heard about a female attorney who had a reputation for taking on difficult divorces. When I met with her, her office was just one big room with a desk and two chairs. A large woman wearing an oversized Mickey Mouse sweatshirt was behind the desk and introduced herself as the attorney. I was a little surprised by her informal attire, but I liked her right away. I gave her my records to look at and she promised she would get back to me as soon as she could.

Soon she called, but the news wasn't good. She informed me that she could not take my case because it would be a conflict of interest. She was part of the law firm that transferred Ed's assets so he could avoid the creditors. I was crushed. She referred me to an attorney, Fred Meyer in Rochester. I met with this man, liked him, hired him, and paid him a retainer fee of $2,000. Unfortunately, the retainer fee was quickly used up and my attorney's bill began heading for the $4,000 mark. To make matters worse, my new attorney wanted me to let my husband keep everything. Obviously, I disagreed. I left that law firm with a large bill and no resolution.

Chapter 6

Men, Lies, and Money

MY BROTHER REFERRED ME TO ANOTHER law office in the Twin Cities that had helped an acquaintance of his, Howe, Irwin and Dorsey law firm. I used Ross Irwin from this law firm and felt I now had a law firm large enough to handle the roadblocks Ed would throw in my path.

My new law firm sprang into action as soon as I supplied them with all the personal and financial records I had, including the monthly income reports from the car wash.

The unfolding web of legal documents, rulings, emails, arguments, arbitrations, depositions, and interrogatories, with a side order of lie after lie, could be a book in itself. I am going to do my best to summarize below, but as you can imagine, a five-year legal battle is deep, murky, and complex.

The attorneys focused on our million-dollar car wash business, and the divorce proceedings dragged on, I was pressured to arbitration by my attorney, Ross Irwin. He told me that an arbitrator has the same power as a judge and arbitration was the only way to end this exhausting process.

He was relentless in his efforts to persuade me to seek arbitration as a means of obtaining a divorce. He told me that he did not know if he could protect me from the rulings of the judge. He even suggested, "The judge might take it upon himself to prosecute you once he learns of the skimming that was occurring at the car wash."

I dug in my heels and resisted. It just didn't feel fair to me.

Then there was the matter of the shady loan from the bank in southern Minnesota that had been set on fire by the VP to cover his sins. This matter was addressed in a formal letter sent by Ed's attorney, Michael Kane, to my representative:

> " . . . *Ed Klein has a good defense to several of the notes running in favor of the State Bank on the grounds that they were forged by a bank officer who, as you will recall, then proceeded to burn down the bank to hide his illegal activities in this file as well as other bank customer files...*"

Once again, Ed was shifting blame and denying his past criminal behavior. Once again, Ed's attorneys continued to cover his tracks. Below are a few excerpts:

[Response from Charles J. Smith Law Office: Certified Civil Trial Specialist]

> "*Mr. Daring has requested that I forward to him copies of the discovery which has been answered by Mr. Klein. I reviewed some of the voluminous discoveries supplied by Mr. Kane. The paper tracks of transfers to avoid lawful claims of creditors are all too evident in this file. Mr. Daring will have something of a field day, I'm afraid, at such time I am compelled to give this information to him.*
> *. . . If I may be blunt, I would like to suggest to both of you gentlemen that you are doing your clients a*

grave disservice by not undertaking every step possible to promptly and expeditiously settle these dissolution proceedings before State Bank/Second Bank of Twin Cities intrudes to set aside whatever it is that the Kleins' had hoped to accomplish. I doubt that I will be able to forestall supplying the information to Mr. Daring which he seeks.

[The formal response from my attorney's office to me on June 14, 1989]

"Dear Jeanie,
As you know, we were recently informed by a letter from Mr. Smith of the $340,000 Promissory Note which Ed Klein personally guaranteed in connection with Acorn Manufacturing. This was the first we heard of this alleged debt. . . ."

" . . . As you also know, this debt could very well render this a "no asset" divorce. The only information we have is that supplied to us by Charles J. Smith in his May 19, 1989, letter. Ed's answers to the Interrogatories do not reveal the existence of this debt."

" . . . We contacted your previous attorney, who confirms that he was indeed under the impression that the debt was resolved and had no reason to tell us about it."

Even as these pieces of information came to light, my attorney continued to push me to go into arbitration. His motive was that he did not want me in a courtroom telling the truth about all the fraudulent activities that were occurring. I finally agreed to seek arbitration as a means to obtain my divorce. I signed the document, Stipulation to be Bound by the Arbitrators Award. On our first meeting, the arbitrator announced, "I will not force the sale of the car wash." I immediately spoke, "How can you say that when you don't even know who owns the car wash?" Everyone in the room remained silent. I felt betrayed.

At one of our arbitration meetings, Ed brought an "appraiser" with him. This stranger had blond hair, medium build and height, and was younger than Ed. Unknown to me at this point, he would reappear in my life. He testified that the car wash was valued at a little over $515,000, which was not accurate. In addition, the "appraiser" wasn't even a certified appraiser. He was a fake. My attorney also felt that the appraisal, which had been done, three years prior, was no longer accurate.

It never ceased to amaze me how Ed could lie and never bat an eye. Here is a more detailed description of a few of my struggles during the five-year slog that was my divorce proceedings. Through it all, I only wanted two things:

1. To be compensated fairly for all of our joint assets.
2. That the truth would prevail.

Inconsistencies and contradictions within Ed's testimonies and documentation continue to grow, including claims that he contributed $8,000 of non-marital funds to our homestead. But when he was questioned again by my attorney, he stated that he contributed $20,000 of non-marital funds to the homestead. His figure was grossly exaggerated. When I demanded that he produce receipts or documents to corroborate the second claim, he couldn't do so.

Ed also claimed that the fourplex apartment building we owned together was not worth more than $120,000. But later, in a financial statement to the courts, he listed the fourplex as having a value of $140,000. Early in our divorce proceedings, Ed stated that his yearly salary was only $15,000. He later recanted that and claimed his yearly income was $36,000. There were many significant contradictions and straight-up lies in the attorney discovery documents furnished by Ed; they were too numerous to list. But

I can say that each contradiction made a large difference in the amount of marital assets to be divided.

My attorney felt we needed to concentrate our efforts on establishing the value of the car wash and insisted we hire a well-known appraiser at the cost of $36,000. I felt this was an extremely high fee, but this man came very highly recommended. My attorney arranged to have a new appraisal done and this one placed the value of the business at $1,161,000.

On January 18, 1989, I had another meeting with my attorney and his legal assistant, and they revealed to me that they could not prove beyond a reasonable doubt that Ed and I owned more than 50 percent of our business. He reminded me that I participated in giving Roger Hammer 50 percent of our business even though I had corporate tax records that stated that Ed and I owned 88 percent. I left the office in a state of intense frustration and anger. When I got home, I immediately wrote my attorney a letter that stated that he did not know what type of an individual he was up against.

It was at this point that I began to realize just how difficult this divorce was going to be and how hard I was going to have to work to bring out the truth.

One of the many things that had frustrated me over the years was the fact that I knew Ed was skimming money from the car wash register. Some people call it "unreported sales," but basically it is the illegal act of not ringing up a customer's sale so the undocumented money could be pocketed by the business owner.

Shortly after my last meeting with my attorney, Mr. Irwin, I made a trip to the car wash. As I stood watching my truck go through the wash cycle, I felt someone walk up beside me. I turned to see a man named Abe Toft, one of our former managers from the car wash. He was clearly surprised to see me there and we talked briefly. Eventually, I mustered up the courage to ask him directly about the skimming that was occurring at our car wash. At first, Abe was evasive, until I reminded him that I had been a cashier at the business and remember putting away as much as $250 a day per Ed's instructions. Abe grew quiet, then responded that it was closer to $350 a day in unreported sales.

When I asked Abe what became of the money, he said it was split three ways. Ed took one-third, Roger pocketed one-third, and he himself took one-third. He stated that he had secretly kept records of the amount he was given. I asked Abe if he would help me by giving my attorney his records of the skimming, or at least talk to my attorney. He said he would.

I felt validated at last.

I had been insisting to Mr. Irwin that Ed was stealing as much as $100,000 a year from under the counter. Now I finally had someone who would confirm those suspicions.

Despite these new revelations, things continued to drag on. There always seemed to be a new obstacle as soon as one was resolved. Soon we were back in the attorney's office undergoing more depositions. During Ed's deposition, my attorney asked him: "Aren't you afraid that Roger Hammer will run away with your assets?" Ed's response was quick and was a true indication of what kind of man he really was:

"You saw how little Roger is, right? I am a lot bigger than him."

During this second round of questioning, my attorney asked Ed again if he ever owned more than 50 percent of the car wash. Again, Ed denied it. Mr. Irwin repeated the question, and again Ed denied it. My attorney quickly countered that he had records that stated otherwise.

Ed shot back just as quickly, "*Well, that 88 percent is wrong.*"

Ed also insisted that he bought the car wash in 1972, before we were married, so I had no legal right to it. Again, he was caught in yet another lie when the tax records revealed the car wash was purchased and paid for *after* our marriage on June 23, 1977. Mr. Irwin produced a copy of Ed's divorce papers from his first marriage in 1976, and they contained no mention of a car wash as an asset.

Later, when we paused for a break, Mr. Irwin took me out of the office and said to me; "Is this the way Ed always is?" I said, "Yes, he's a pretty good liar, isn't he?" Mr. Irwin shook his head in disgust, "No, he's actually a terrible liar and it is all too obvious. He has now told three different versions! He can't keep his stories straight!"

Knowing my legal bills were rising and my income was dwindling, I listed my original home for sale. It sold quickly, and the new owners were to take possession on May 31, 1989. Unfortunately, I never saw any of the money from the sale of my house. The check had been issued in both of our names and I refused to endorse it. At a much later date, Ed's attorney convinced my realtor to send *him* the check so he could apply it to Ed's legal bills.

In the second week of March 1989, I received a phone call from my attorney's legal assistant informing me that my divorce had been canceled for March 27 and reassigned June 19, 1989. It felt like there was no end in sight. In the end, our divorce was pushed back and rescheduled five more times.

On May 2, 1989, my attorney informed me that the car wash's former manager, Abe Toft, was not willing to testify unless he was subpoenaed into court. The rumor around town was that Ed had paid Abe a visit and threatened to "run him out of business" if he testified. It was one defeat, and one dead end, after another.

By this time, my attorney was beginning to see that trying to collect money from Ed was going to be a huge struggle. We had other assets, namely our house in Forest Park and our fourplex rental, but he refused to go after those assets on my behalf because my attorney bill was "already too high."

Ultimately, Ed did admit to the skimming during an arbitration hearing, but he demanded it not be recorded, so the attorneys and the arbitrator agreed to turn the recorder off. His confession made me feel a little more validated, but it did nothing to help in the fair division of our assets.

My attorney and I left the arbitrator's office afterward and went straight back to his office. Once there, Mr. Irwin commented on the huge amount of money that Ed had been skimming from the car wash business and referred to it all as Ed's "Golden Goose."

"*Everyone* should have a 'Golden Goose' that lays 'Golden Eggs,'" he absently commented to me. It wasn't until many years later that he revealed to me that his personal "Golden Goose" was the fact that he didn't report all his income.

The inconsistencies in the divorce interrogatories continued. Ed continued to undervalue our joint assets and to lie about any money he was supposedly sending me. Each inconsistency lowered our marital assets and what fair compensation I should have coming to me would have been decreased. I could never shake the uneasy feeling that Ed was always one step ahead of me. He seemed committed to destroying my life and leaving me with nothing. He was like an invasive weed that kept wrapping new roots around me as soon as I whacked one off.

On our last day of arbitration, my attorney hit his fist forcefully on his desk, leaned over, and pointed a finger at me. He shocked me by threatening, "I will not do another thing for you until you agree to the terms of the arbitration." He then ushered me in to another room where the arbitrator and Ed's attorney were waiting. Mr. Irwin said, "Jeanie will agree to the terms of arbitration." The arbitrator said, "What protection do we have from Jeanie if she is subpoenaed to Court, and she tells the truth?" Mr. Irwin said, "You have nothing to worry about, all the records have been pulled from the courthouse and destroyed, it is her word against ours."

I felt so betrayed.

With my southern Minnesota farm sold, I began the long process of moving to my farm in North Town on May 31. My daughter and I moved ourselves by using my horse trailer to haul furniture as well as horses. All told, we made ten round trips from southern Minnesota to northern Minnesota. Each trip was 500 miles. But at least there was now some geographic distance between myself and the man who seemed hell-bent on making my life miserable.

My divorce settlement was eventually resolved and finalized on January 7, 1991. As part of the final agreement, I was awarded monthly lease payments from Ed, and he was free to continue to manage the car wash. It sounded good on paper, but in reality, I was forced to file several Unlawful Detainers to collect my money, which also increased my attorney costs even more. As if trying to deliver one final blow of retaliation, I later found out that Ed and his bar waitress girlfriend flew to Las Vegas on New Year's Eve 1991 and got married, even though he and I were not yet legally divorced.

This five-year marathon to be free from a toxic and cruel man left me broke and broken. I was in debt up to my ears. I had $100,000 in attorney fees, and still owed my brother, Robert, the $40,000 that he had loaned me to pay for my North Town farm. Struggling to make ends meet, I had already sold everything I could, except my horses. This included selling my beautiful new pick-up truck and horse trailer. The only asset that was 100 percent mine was my horses. I was working two jobs so I could take care of myself, my daughter, and my horses. There was never any extra money.

During these bleak times, I could no longer compete in my endurance rides, even though they had always brought me much happiness. But I still clung to the dream that one day I would be competing again in the endurance rides.

When my divorce finally went through, my brother stopped by the farm with a single rose and said, "Congratulations on your divorce."

I said, "Congratulations for what, the hell of my life is just beginning?"

Thankfully, there were bright spots in my life as well. I was now working full-time at the North Town Medical Clinic and my salary had gone up to $8.50 an hour. Money was still tight, and I was trying my best to support my horses, which had doubled in numbers. Most of my horses were registered thoroughbreds and I was getting a few foals every spring. I needed to make more money, so I applied for casual positions in the emergency room at a major hospital thirty miles from my house. Still, money leaked out of my checkbook as fast as I could put it in.

Another blessing was that my daughter had graduated from an Honors Program in Psychology, and had met her future husband, Dean. I was so proud of her and knew she and Dean were a great couple. They were married in December of 1992, and it was a beautiful ceremony.

In November of 1992, I requested all my records from the attorney in south Minneapolis. His secretary collected several boxes and called me to tell me they were ready. My sister lived in the Metro and offered to go over to their office and retrieve them. Ultimately, she transported five boxes of paperwork and files to my home in North Town. When I saw how much paper there was, I was shocked. Then I realized that I had not only scored my divorce records, but also all my attorney's records on my case.

The five boxes contained arbitration agreements, letters of correspondence between the attorneys, interrogations, motions, trial memorandums, private emails between attorneys on both sides, and much more. It was a paper trail of proof, never meant for my eyes, that the lawyers had plotted to protect my ex-husband.

Among the many files and paperwork, I found a letter written by Ed's attorney to the real estate office that handled the sale of my homestead. The letter requested that the real estate attorney make arrangements to have the money from the sale of property sent directly to Ed's attorney and cut me out completely. This confirmed the rumor that I had heard about how Ed was not paying his attorney at all. I suspect that his attorney knew that the only way he would see any money from this divorce fiasco was if he made arrangements to take mine. I knew Ed well enough to know he had no intentions of ever paying his bill.

My initial joy surrounding this unplanned stroke of luck quickly faded when I realized that being in possession of these damning files could be a curse as well. My gut instinct was that someone would come looking for these records because I am certain I was not ever meant to have them. Several attorneys and Ed would not be pleased that I was now in possession of a powerhouse of information.

And they would want it back.

I did not know what to do next with these boxes of incriminating papers, so I hid them at several different friends' houses for safekeeping. There was one letter that I pulled from the boxes. This was the letter that my ex-husband's attorney wrote to my real estate agency requesting that the check from the sale of my farm be sent to him. I never had endorsed that check over to him. To this day, I believe it was these boxes of incriminating records that set a series of ominous events into motion.

In the summer of 1993. I went to Rochester to conciliation court. I had filed a claim against Ed, my ex-husband, for the sum of $4500. This amount was granted to me in my divorce decree and had never been paid. Ed came to court assisted by his wife and told a story of hardship. The court ruled in my favor, and I was granted a judgment for the money. The court managed to take $500 out of Ed's checking account. This would have made Ed furious and his previous statement to me, "You will pay for this," was set into motion.

After conciliation court and before I left Rochester, I went over to the office of Ed's attorney. I walked into his office and told his secretary that I had a letter for him. It was his letter that he had written my real estate office requesting my money. He began screaming at me to get out of there, so I quickly left the office and drove out of Rochester. He was furious with me, and I can only assume he contacted my attorney asking how I manage to have that letter.

Chapter 7

Jesus Take the Wheel

THEY SAY HINDSIGHT IS 20/20, AND NOW, when I look back on certain things that led up to the weeks before Pearl's murder, there were strange things that happened to which I should have paid closer attention. They were red flags that I should have heeded and hints to the danger that was yet to come.

Despite being officially divorced from Ed, I always felt he was not far away from me. Lurking. Waiting. Some may have called it paranoia, but I know now that it was my intuition warning me.

In October 1993, I borrowed a two-horse trailer from a friend and hooked it up to my truck, with the intention of getting out of town for a while and clearing my head. My plan was to head to Oklahoma to pick up two horses from a racetrack and spend some quality time learning from the trainer.

Before I set off on my cross-country road trip, I dropped my 1984 pickup at my brother's auto dealership to be thoroughly checked over by the mechanics. I needed to have peace of mind that there would be no issues on the way. After my vehicle was checked out and found to be mechanically sound including an oil change, I made plans for my trip. On October 28, I stopped at a gas station not far from my home, filled up both of my gas tanks, and hit the road.

My first destination was to be my dear friend Abby's house in Rochester. The plan was for us to spend the evening chatting and catching up before getting on the road together the next morning. She had told me ahead of time that she would likely not be home yet when I arrived, but to go ahead and make myself comfortable in her house. Abby had a big golden retriever who had been trained not to bark. He was very glad to see me and expressed his delight at a new human visitor with nothing more than a tail wag. Not long after I arrived, Abby came home, and we giggled and chatted while she gave me the grand tour of the remodeling she recently done in her lovely home. Part of the remodel was a new bedroom downstairs. Usually, when I stayed at her house, I took the upstairs guest bedroom that faced her driveway. For some reason, the thought of staying in my usual room wasn't sitting well with me and I couldn't shake an uneasy feeling. I took the new bedroom downstairs under the guise that I wanted to "test out" the new room.

Even though Abby was my friend, I was very aware that her close friend David hung out with Ed at the car wash. I knew it was very probable that Abby would have mentioned to David that I was coming and that he, in turn, would have mentioned it to Ed. It was no secret to any of our old friends and acquaintances from Rochester how bitter our divorce had been. That night, I locked the doors of my truck but neglected to lock the slider on the back window. Looking back, I wish I had.

In the morning, Abby and I jumped into my truck and began the long drive to Oklahoma City towing my trailer. As I pulled out of her driveway, I immediately noticed that my truck just didn't run right. When you rely on your truck for work and life, you know its' every creak, squeak, and quirk. I could immediately sense a difference in the way it drove and how the engine sounded. Even though we were pulling a trailer, there was more than the normal resistance.

The engine also felt like it lacked power and was working overtime to keep a steady speed. Despite my concerns, we continued on.

About 100 miles into our drive, I noticed my gas gauge was going down very, very fast. Way too fast. My truck was a gas guzzler, but even this was out of the ordinary. Alarmed, we pulled over at a safe spot alongside the road and, as I got out of my vehicle, I could smell burning oil. When I grabbed the hood release so I could investigate the smell, it fell off right in my hand. This was **not** normal. Despite the broken latch, I was able to get my hood up. I could see spilled oil on top of the engine, and it was smoking and bubbling. Knowing that my vehicle had just had an oil change, I dismissed it as sloppy mechanics and shut the hood. Abby suggested we go back and get her truck, but we were so far into our trip that backtracking didn't sound like a good option.

Silently, I wondered if I had gotten bad gas at my last stop, but the thought that someone had tampered with my vehicle wasn't far from my mind either. The fact that my truck had been unattended all night, and that Abby's dog would not have barked even if there were strangers tampering with my vehicle, kept swirling around in my brain. I said nothing of my worries and tried to concentrate on getting to Oklahoma.

It wasn't farfetched to suspect Ed of ordering some of his more easy-to-manipulate employees to sabotage my truck. He had what I would call "two sides." He was charming and gracious to those who didn't know him well. But, as someone who was once close to him, I knew of his "other side"...his darker side. The knowledge of what he could be capable of didn't make it far-fetched that maybe he would orchestrate something devious like sabotaging my vehicle.

I remembered a time while Ed and I were dating, and I went to the car wash to visit him. As I walked up to Ed, his first wife was just driving away. With a dark look on his face, he commented, "She won't be bringing that car in here again." When I inquired what he meant, Ed responded with a sly smile, "Because I fixed' it."

Ed had done his special "fix-it job" on my vehicle in the past as well. The last time I had taken my car to the Full-Service Car Wash for a wash and an oil change, my son (who worked there) informed me that Ed had "personally" worked on my car. Days later, when the car started acting up, I took it to the dealership for repair and was told that the positive battery cable had a slit in it and the distributor cap had several slits. After that, I never took my vehicle back to the car wash.

After we got back on the road, my truck ran fair. As we pulled into Kansas City, Kansas, my tailpipe fell off with a loud bang. We circled back around to retrieve it and threw it into the bed of my pickup. It was a noisier drive now that we were minus a tailpipe, but at least the truck was still running somewhat decently.

It was late in the afternoon when we arrived in Oklahoma City. Luckily, we found our motel and it didn't look too terrible. We unloaded our luggage and made plans to visit Remington Park in the morning to watch the horses run. We spent the rest of the day touring Oklahoma City and enjoying our time under less stressful circumstances. We visited the National Cowboy and Western Heritage Museum.

The next day, we went back to Remington Park, and it was good to see my horses, along with their trainer, doing their workouts and test runs. I told our trainer, John Logan, we would be over early the next morning to load horses for the journey back. He warned us that there was a snowstorm brewing in Minnesota and we needed to plan our trip accordingly. Truthfully, the information didn't bother me since I was very used to driving in snowy Minnesota weather.

The next morning, we loaded the horses in my trailer and prepared for a long trip back. Before entering the freeway at the north edge of Oklahoma City, I stopped once again to fill both gas tanks. My front tank was the larger tank; my back tank was the smaller reserve tank. Typically, I would run the front tank first; when it became low on fuel, I would switch to the smaller reserve tank.

As I started to get in my truck, I heard a very commanding voice inside my brain. It was a voice that caught my attention and startled me with its clarity. It was not an audible voice . . . it was more a stroke of intuition. The words I heard, clear as day, instructed me to run my **back** gas tank first. I remember glancing around behind me, fully expecting to see a human.

There was no one. My faith tells me, it was a message from God.

But instead of being alarmed, I felt a strange sense of peace and found myself fully trusting the instructions. I climbed back into my truck and switched immediately to the back gas tank. I also remember Abby looking at me in surprise since she was used to my normal process. I commented to her that I had decided to use the back gas tank *first* and left it at that. She stared at me for a moment, but eventually just shrugged her shoulders and said, "Okay."

On the interstate, my truck engine was once again roaring and straining. Cars were passing as though we were standing still, and we could only top out at 40 mph on the freeway. My truck would not pick up speed either, even when we were going downhill. Abby commented that she was afraid that we were going too slow and were causing a hazard on the interstate. There was obviously something not right with my vehicle. But we plowed forward anyway, intent on getting back to Minnesota ahead of the snowstorm.

As I was coaxing my trusty vehicle along, my muffler suddenly changed sounds and began emitting a low, moaning sound. It kept getting louder, and the dread began rising in my chest.

It was as if my truck was failing one piece at a time.

Pushing better judgment aside, I gritted my teeth, clenched the steering wheel until my knuckles turned white, and continued at our snail's pace for about 40 minutes more. Sadly, my truck seemed done for when the engine died without warning. We coasted over to the side of the road and did our best to restart the engine. After a couple of tries, I was able to get it started, but once again things just did not feel right. Within a block, the engine died again, and we were forced to pull over off the interstate. As I climbed out, I could hear a loud hissing noise coming from the back of my vehicle. The metal on the side of my truck was burning hot to the touch and a hissing noise was coming from the back gas tank. I was truly afraid it was about to explode.

Being stranded on the side of the road on a major interstate highway is not for the faint of heart. Traffic was zipping by us so fast that cars were a blur, and it was not safe to unload our horses. Abby and I stood beside the trailer with lead ropes in hand just in case we would have to unload in an emergency. I was fully expecting flames to start licking the side of my truck at any moment.

It took about 30 minutes for the hissing sound in my gas tank to stop making noises and even longer for my heart rate to go back to slightly normal. Tentatively, I turned the gas cap to release the steam from the tank. I could see what appeared to be a gas station in the distance and I prayed I could limp my truck a mile down the road to get some mechanical help. Not sure if that back gas tank was safe anymore, I switched to the front tank and slowly drove to the station. I was appalled when we found no mechanic on duty, and the staff at the station could not help us. It was one more frustrating roadblock in a series of unexplained events.

Abby and I decided to take the time needed to wire my tailpipe back on. I wasn't sure if the missing tailpipe was causing a problem, but I wasn't willing to take the chance. As I crawled under the truck, I noticed that the brackets that held my tailpipe in place were all intact. No broken brackets meant that the tailpipe should have stayed on. Things were getting worse by the minute.

We were told that there was another gas station about ten miles up the road, so we slowly made our way there. Upon arrival, we parked, unhitched the horse trailer, and paid the mechanic on duty to put my truck up on the hoist. Within minutes, what he discovered made my blood run cold. My muffler had a seam split wide open, and its close proximity to the back gas tank made the gas inside heat to the point of being cooked. The boiling gas had gone into the engine and killed the engine on the interstate. The realization hit me that, if I had been running off my larger front gas tank as I normally would, I would have been driving a ticking time bomb. The larger volume of gas would have kept my vehicle driving until it was too late, and we all would have been killed in one epic and terrifying fireball explosion. It was a sickening and sobering realization. This chain of events was not likely a "fluke" or a freak accident.

The mechanic put on a new muffler, reattached my tailpipe, and assured us we would not blow up. It was not my first choice to climb back in that vehicle and hitch the horse trailer to head home, but we really had no other choice. As we continued on our journey, my truck still had no pulling power, and I could only coax it to go about 40 mph. I knew . . . we both knew . . . that it was going to be a long drive back.

As we drove in shocked silence, I had plenty of time to think and wonder who had sabotaged my truck. By the grace of God, we arrived in Minnesota just as a snowstorm was hitting. Abby called David from a phone at a restaurant and asked him to pick her up at Interstate 90, so I didn't have to try to navigate the slippery side roads to take her home. As I passed through Minneapolis, I was unlucky enough to hit prime rush hour traffic, which ratcheted up my anxiety even more. Gripping the steering wheel like my life depended on it (because it did), I continued driving in the snowstorm all by myself at a top speed of 35 mph. Just me and my two scared horses in the trailer.

To add another layer of "crazy" to this trip was the fact that, not only was it a Friday night, but it was also the day before deer hunting opener, so the traffic was insane. Finally, after what felt like an eternity, I arrived in the city of Brainerd, which meant I was only about 30 miles from home. That final stretch of road to home was incredibly slippery; even being in four-wheel drive wasn't helping much. As I approached my driveway, I could see a big snowdrift blocking the entrance. I swung wide, stepped on the gas, and busted my way through the big drift.

There was no pile of snow on the earth big enough to keep me from the safety of my home.

Engine roaring in protest, I forced my vehicle through the deep snow and up to my barn. By then it was midnight, and the horses were hungry and ready to get out of the trailer. To say I was exhausted was an understatement, but their care came first. I exercised them for a few minutes in a large pen before blanketing them up and bedding them down in a stall with grain, hay, and water. Finally, I collapsed into my bed for a night of fitful sleep.

Two days later, I had regained my composure enough to take my truck *back* to the auto dealership to be checked for a second time. I told the mechanic on duty at the auto dealership about all the mechanical failures I had just experienced on a truck that had supposedly been given a clean bill of health just days before. After a thorough inspection, I was told that my distributor cap and wires were badly damaged, and my positive battery cable had a slit in it. I was also told that I needed a new manifold, new tie rods, and a new spare tire, since the rubber had been nearly burned off by my boiling gas tank and the heat from my muffler. I picked up my truck a few days later and drove it home, but I could tell something was still not right.

The next day, I took my truck back to the auto dealership for the third time. When the mechanic got in, he noticed my truck did not roll even though I had parked on a slight incline, and it was in neutral. This was not normal.

Once the truck was on the hoist, I was told that "someone" had tightened my brake drums to the point where they were causing drag. On top of everything else that needed to be replaced, I was told I needed new brake drums, too. In total, the repairs cost me over $3,000 for a vehicle that had been checked and approved for travel before I even left northern Minnesota. If the intention was to have me and my truck blow up 800 miles from home, there was only one man I knew that would have the motive and desire to make that happen. To this day, I am convinced that I was not supposed to return to Minnesota.

And the strange situations and coincidences were about to escalate even more.

Chapter 8

Hunter or the Hunted

After my near-death experience between Minnesota and Oklahoma, I was not overly anxious to leave home. Typically, I was an avid deer hunter, but that year my heart just wasn't in it. Feeling uneasy about life in general, I opted to skip deer hunting that year and stay close to my farm. As soon as my son, William was old enough to hunt, he joined Ed and I at my brother's hunting shack. William lived to hunt deer and would spend as much time as he could at the hunting shack.

In Minnesota, deer hunting is a big deal. The season starts the first weekend in November and lasts two weeks. During this time, every county for miles is filled with armed men and women wearing blaze-orange hunting attire. One of the highlights of deer hunting for our hunting party was sitting around and listening to all the deer stories of the day. Whenever someone shot a deer, they would keep a log of their name, where they shot the deer, its gender, and the date. Personally, I loved the peace and quiet of the woods, watching the birds, especially the chickadees, and seeing all the little animals of the forest.

Veteran hunters all knew the unwritten code about respecting other hunters' property, favorite spots, and hunting shacks, even if they happen to be on state land. It is rare to see a stranger in your designated hunting area unless they are lost or confused. During my 35 years of hunting in our hunting party's chosen spot, I never saw any other hunters on our land.

It was the last weekend of the 1993 deer hunting season in our territory, and I had decided against going. I made the excuse of being too busy that final weekend. Even though I bowed out, my nephew, Gus, went as usual and claimed his "spot" in his father's prime hunting shack.

The road that leads back to our chosen hunting area is very rough and rugged and can only be traveled with a modified "monster truck" with a lift kit that could navigate the wild terrain. There were two of these "hunting trucks" in our hunting party and we always traveled to the deer camp in pairs. When one truck got hung up on a stump or stuck in the mud, the second truck would be available to pull it free. This was a common occurrence for our hunting party, so everyone planned accordingly. Part of me would miss the camaraderie and thrill of hunting season, but it was a choice that I would soon be grateful to have made.

After the hunting season of 1993 ended, my nephew revealed to me that things had been very different this season. For the first time in many years, two strange men were spotted hunting out of *my* stand, the stand close to the shack that I routinely hunted in every season. Gus shared that not only were these strangers hunting without permission, but he also felt they did not look or act like typical hunters. They carried small caliber rifles that were not suitable for bringing down big game like a whitetail. One of the men shot a little fawn and removed only the loin. A typical hunter would have taken the entire fawn with him. But, because our party hunted public land instead of private land, there was little they could do other than tell these strangers to go find a different place to hunt.

Gus saw them again on the last day of hunting but, instead of avoiding our area as they were asked to do, they were lurking even closer to the deer hunting shack. My nephew spotted them again when he was in one of the crappiest places a person could be when being approached by strangers—**in the outhouse.**

Through the cracks in the outhouse wall, Gus told me he watched the men walking quietly towards the shack. As he watched, it dawned on him that he had left his rifle leaning against the main shack. Basically, he was unarmed and vulnerable, with his pants around his ankles.

One of the strangers pounded on the door of the deer shack with his fist. The wife of one of our hunting companions, Faith, answered the door. The men proceeded to ask angrily who the owner of the hunting shack was, and Faith responded that it belonged to her husband. The men were clearly agitated and unhappy but turned abruptly and left, never to be seen again.

Weeks later, when Gus relayed the story to me, I had a sickening feeling in my stomach. I suspect that those men were not hunting deer that day.

It took me nearly 25 years to press Gus for more details of that day. Even though decades had passed, his description of the strangers was still strong and clear as the day he saw them in 1993. The taller man appeared to be the leader. He was around six feet tall, with a thin build and a narrow face. His hair was blondish, greasy, long, and unwashed. His appearance was dirty and disheveled and included a scraggly beard. He wore faded jeans and a faded orange sweatshirt. He had a deer-hunting-orange stocking cap, but his gloves were not orange in color. He held his gun in his left hand.

The second man was shorter in height and medium build. His appearance was the opposite of the other man. He was clean-cut, with short brown hair and short sideburns. His clothing consisted of a red plaid long-sleeve shirt with an orange vest over the top. He also wore jeans that were not faded and appeared new. His gloves were not orange and on his head was a baseball-type cap that was also not orange. He carried his rifle on his right shoulder in a sling.

Even after all these years, Gus said that the memory of these suspicious strangers was so burned into his brain that, from then on, he never left his rifle behind, no matter where he was in deer camp. Especially, when he was in the outhouse! He also felt these men were up to no good and likely looking for someone. My guess was that it was *me* they were after.

I have never returned to the deer camp since that encounter. It was the second warning that I should have seen but did not. A little over a month later, my friend and neighbor was dead.

And I believe it was supposed to be me.

Chapter 9

The Thread That
Bound Us Together

PEARL JUSTICE WAS A WONDERFUL WOMAN. Wise and kind, she was a giver of her time, a listening ear, and the creator of delicious baked treats.

We first met when I was in high school and worked at a local resort during the summer months. Pearl was the cook, and I was a new waitress. We became good friends in that hot kitchen while serving vacationing families from all over the country.

Back in those days, waitresses at the resort were not allowed to write down any of the orders; we had to memorize them all. Then we had to take those memorized orders and give them to the cook verbally. If we had six people for breakfast, we had to remember how each one wanted their eggs and if they wanted sausage or bacon. Pearl was very patient with me as I fumbled and stumbled through the first weeks of my new employment.

As time went on, I got better at my job and Pearl was a wonderful coworker who always had a smile on her face. I will never forget the day Pearl made a gallon of mayonnaise, a task that took her most of the day. Once finished, she asked me to take the jar of newly made condiment to the cooler. When I picked up the jar and reached for the door of the cooler, the jar slipped from my hands and smashed onto the tile floor. Devastated and embarrassed, I shuffled into the kitchen to confess to my friend that I had just undone almost a whole day's work.

But I didn't need to apologize—she had obviously heard the crash. But instead of being angry, she just smiled and never said a word. That was what Pearl was like: calm, forgiving, and understanding. I worked all summer with Pearl, and she made my job much easier and joyful.

Eventually, we drifted apart when I graduated, moved away from the area, and began living a busy adult life. Little did I know that, in 30-odd years, our paths would cross again.

In the spring of 1989, my daughter Sherry and I made the move from Rochester to North Town. I had bought a farm from my brother, Robert, who had assured me that it was a good investment. My new property had a former life as an old dairy farm, and it included a huge barn, a 100-foot pole shed, a 10-car garage, and 325 acres. The house has been completely remodeled as well. It felt like heaven for me and all my horses.

It was a surprise and delight to see that my new neighbor, who was one driveway south of me, was my old friend Pearl. When she heard that I had moved in next door, she came to see me with a plateful of homemade donuts. They were delicious, and it was nice to see her again.

Pearl was a good person who deserved many good things in life, but one thing she did not deserve was to be brutally murdered in her own home. This event was made even more haunting because I firmly believe that the intruders' intended mark was supposed to be **me**.

Chapter 10

Remembering

THE TRUTH OF THE EVENTS OF THAT night continued to elude me and trying to piece them all together continued to be a struggle.

I knew something bad had happened . . . I just couldn't reach the dark recesses of my mind to retrieve the memory of what I had witnessed. It took five long months for the fog in my brain, about the night Pearl died, to finally clear. In May of 1994, I happened to run into Pearl's daughter-in-law, Karen, at the gas station when I was there to fill my gas tanks. She approached me and we chatted. I told her I was taking some of my horses to Missouri for training and I was looking forward to getting out of town for a bit.

Karen told me to have a safe trip. I replied that I would, since I wasn't going anywhere near where my ex-husband lived, so he wouldn't be able to rig my truck to explode again.

Then her demeanor shifted unexpectedly. She began to ask me a series of odd questions, including asking if my ex-husband knew where I lived and if he knew what color my house was. Her questions were disturbing, and they truly frightened me. We parted ways and I went back home to finish packing.

Once home, I couldn't shake the confusion about her line of questioning, and it quickly turned to anger. I called Karen and screamed at her, "**Why?**"

WHY are you asking me these things?

Does it have to do with Pearl's death?

Did she die from a heart attack while baking and, when she fell, her clothes caught on fire?

Why are you asking these things?

The questions were flying out of my mouth so fast I could barely catch my breath. Karen was quiet for a moment, then she responded, "No, *the baking and heart attack scenario is just what we want everyone to believe.*"

I was crushed, and the reality of that horrible night was starting to take a grip on my memory again. The rest of our conversation was blank to me because my mind and heart were both racing. Once on the road to Missouri, I had a long time to think, and memories of the details of that night began to flood back. By the time I reached my destination, I had remembered the two men at Pearl's with enough clarity to let me know it was not all a dream after all. It was a real-life nightmare.

Among the memories that became clear, was the fact that I knew both men on the deck of Pearl's house that night. The distinctively short man was indeed Roger, an associate of Ed's. His height and stature were very distinctive and there was no doubt in my mind it was him.

The second man resembled one of Ed's sons, but it finally dawned on me that he was the same man who showed up at my divorce proceedings years before, claiming to be an appraiser (which he was not). He, too, was a crony of my ex-husband's. The revelation of their identities only cemented what I already knew. These men, under the direction of someone who had great influence over them (my ex-husband), went to the wrong house looking for the incriminating attorney documents. It was supposed to be *me*. Remembering these details was almost too much to bear. But it made me even more determined to seek justice for Pearl.

When I returned to Minnesota, I called Karen again and asked her who the lead investigator was for the fire at Pearl's. That same day, I made an appointment with Deputy Al Lang and took my friend, Clarice with me. It was a good thing I had her with me because I sobbed the whole way to Brainerd.

I did my best to explain my story to the deputy, but I couldn't stop crying and I knew I wasn't making a good impression. Even though the memories and facts of that night were clear, I couldn't articulate them. I'm sure I came across as hysterical and incoherent. During the moments when I could calm myself, Deputy Lang would question me. I tried my best to answer, but my thoughts and words kept getting jumbled.

In my calmer moments, I was able to tell him about the odd flicker of light that I'd seen through Pearl's window as I drove past her driveway that night. He pressed me for details. He asked about the size of the light, and I told him that it wasn't a flashlight, but possibly the brief flare of a matchstick.

1. The deputy was as patient as he could be, but I could tell he was skeptical about my recounting of that evening and did not consider me a reliable witness. I had assumed the police department was still investigating the murder, but I was crushed when they told me the case had been ruled as an accidental death and was going to be considered a Closed Case. Not only was I furious, but the reality that I was still not safe was crippling me emotionally.

The witness believed that her ex-husband may have had someone come to the area to kill her. She believed that they came for her but went to the wrong house. When asked, the witness revealed that her ex had never made any overt threats to her or assaulted her. The witness also stated that she did not remember any of the details of the night in question until recently.

[Excerpt from the Sparrow County Investigator's Report on 10/19/94]

Later, at home, I wrote a letter to the staffing nurse at the hospital requesting a copy of my work schedule from December. I was determined to begin compiling proof that I was home at midnight on the night of December 22, 1993. Deputy Lang said he would follow up and call me, but I never heard from him again. He also left out of his report any mention of the flicker of light I witnessed that night even though we had talked about it at length.

I called him again after I checked my work schedule and told him that Pearl had died 15 minutes after midnight on December 22, 1993. That information was never noted in any of his reports.

Several days later, I called the fire marshal of Sparrow County and tried to relay my story to him. As soon as I mentioned that I was the neighbor of Pearl Justice and I had seen two men at her house the night she died, he began shouting angrily at me.

"Give me their names and who they were!" he demanded.

I was so shocked and intimidated by his response, I hung up in a panic. Once again, I felt dismissed and written off by a man in a position of power. Gradually, pieces of that fateful night began to filter back into my memory. Several weeks after my failed conversation with the fire marshal, I was out in my barn cleaning a water tank. From out of nowhere, the vision of the fireball blast at Pearl's hit me like a ton of bricks. I could clearly see Roger shouting at the other man, "This isn't Jeanie's house! You didn't have to do that! She was just an old woman!"

The memory of that horrible scene sapped my energy and reduced me to tears. I sobbed so hard that my hair became wet with sweat. The sudden return of this memory was so horrifying, I couldn't catch my breath and repeatedly choked on my own secretions. I was certain I was going to pass out. These moments also amplified my feelings of being very, very alone and very afraid.

The memory also validated that these men were after me . . . and that realization terrified me. Later in the day, after I had calmed down, two of my dear friends came by and I shared my new memory and the clarity of it. I took them into the pen where I was standing that night to show them that I had a clear line of sight to the back of Pearl's home. They both agreed that, even though it was now summer, and the trees were full of leaves, they could clearly see Pearl's back deck.

For months, I slept with a loaded rifle with "one in the chamber." I spent time practicing flying out of bed and into the "ready to shoot" position at the top of the stairs. I told my children to never come upstairs when I was sleeping because my nerves were on such high alert that I was afraid of what I might accidentally do.

Little by little, more details of that night became clearer and only increased the level of anxiety in my life. I was filled with fear at the knowledge that these men were still "out there" and they now knew exactly where I lived. If a vehicle on the highway slowed down, I would panic in fear. Once I was in the barn when I saw a truck drive into my yard, I hid in the barn until the truck was gone. In desperation, I prayed to God to give me direction and show me the safe path that I needed to take. I repeated this prayer often.

Three weeks after that, I awoke full of energy and vigor. It was a beautiful day and the sun's rays warmed me as I stood by my bed. Then, I felt something that I can only describe as God's arms. His arms wrapped around me, gently sat me down on my bed, and his words were clear as day.

"My dear, you don't have to move your horses. You don't have to move your stuff. You do not need to know where you are going."

I knew this message was exactly what I needed to know, but at that moment, it didn't make sense to me.

Three weeks later, I was having a garage sale and an unfamiliar woman came up to me and introduced herself. She said, "I hear you would like to get away for the winter. We would love to rent your house." I asked her if I could leave my possessions and she said, "As long as you don't mind us using some of them" I then asked if she would be willing to care for my horses and she said, "Yes! Just tell us what to do!"

God's words had come true. I didn't need my stuff and I didn't need to know where I was going.

Despite God's reassurance, I still feared for my life and felt that I needed to get out of town. I stayed in town long enough to vote in early November, and then, I just left as fast as I could. The fact that deer hunting season was the following weekend weighed heavily on my mind as well. I was fearful that the same ominous duo that infiltrated the deer camp the year before would return, looking for me.

Before I left town, I got in touch with a television station and an investigative team down in the Metro and begged them to investigate the murder of my neighbor. My mistake was not waiting for them to come to town to follow up.

Later, I was told that they did indeed come to North Town and began checking into my claims. Since I was not there to defend myself, they were met with resistance and silence. They were even told that I made all of this up to get attention. I spent that fall and winter hiding in Missouri and living in a 12-foot camper that I had rented for $50 a month. My tiny little abode was next to a horse training center where I was able to get work. The camper had electricity, but no running water or heat. But I felt safe since no one except my kids knew where I was living. My little camper was hidden inside an old, unused barn. This not only gave me shelter from the wind, but it also gave me an added layer of privacy.

During my time in hiding, I spent hours writing down my account of what happened on December 22nd. When I look back on these writings now, 28 years later, it pains me to see how wounded, fragile, and troubled I was that winter. But my new simple life was like balm for my wounded soul and slowly I started feeling courageous enough to come back to my farm in North Town.

Even after so much time had passed, bits and pieces of the details of that night kept popping up. Some were comforting, some made me sob for hours. I returned to Minnesota in the spring of 1995, and my anxiety started building before I had even crossed the border into the state. These feelings were compounded by my knowing that there was not a police investigation, and that there needed to be.

I made an appointment with the County Attorney and took my cousin, Amber, with me. I tried my hardest to tell him what I needed to say about that horrible night at Pearl's house, but I kept crying so hard I couldn't speak. I struggled and struggled to get the words out but couldn't.

Finally, in frustration, the County Attorney asked me, "What is it that you want to see happen?"

Amber answered for me and said, "She wants you to reopen the case involving the death of Pearl Justice. He said nothing further other than to agree to send me all the information available regarding Pearl's case.

When the packet of documents arrived, I called my nephew to come and sit with me while I read through everything. To my surprise, the police report of the fire scene noted that there were spent matchsticks found all over Pearl's house.

That explained the flicker of light I had seen through the window the night of December 22, 1993. The reports also mentioned the presence in Pearl's kitchen of a huge garbage bag that was filled with all of her important paperwork and documents. Included in this bag were things like tax statements and her husband's death certificate: things she would never throw out, so they had no place in a garbage bag. Based on this new information, I knew in my heart that Pearl had, in fact, been in bed sleeping when she was awakened by the intruders. I also knew the men, thinking they were at my house, were gathering up any official documents that could be the damning attorneys' records.

Sparrow County law enforcement had ruled that Pearl's demise was an "undetermined cardiac arrest." Even though Karen reported that there were two pieces of her mother-in-law's jewelry missing and an unexplained ten boxes of stick matches found in the house after Pearl died, law enforcement ruled it a closed case. In their minds, Pearl was just a frail 87-year-old woman who fell, hit her head, and set herself on fire. With no other evidence to the contrary, there was little to do after the preliminary investigation than to close the case.

Deputy Al Lang attended the autopsy and was told at that time that Pearl had died of an "undetermined cardiac arrest." By medical standards, "cardiac arrest" is when a heart completely stops and is different from a heart attack. Unfortunately, Deputy Lang assumed that they were one and the same and that she had simply died of a heart attack. He then, in turn, reported to the Fire Marshal that death was due to "heart attack."

To me, the inconsistencies and red flags were crystal clear. I know now it was because I could see the whole picture. It was a complete story of dishonest and ruthless men who had a motive for murder.

I tried to encourage Karen and Pearl's son to pursue my suspicions with me, but she indicated that the family did not want to kick the hornet's nest and insist on an in-depth investigation. She was fearful that her mother-in-law's murder was the result of an ugly land dispute, and they were worried about further retaliation.

I was all alone on my quest for justice for Pearl.

Chapter 11

No Justice for Pearl

LIFE CONTINUED TO BE A STRUGGLE for me, but my horses kept me going. I needed them and they needed me. All the money I earned from nursing went for my horses. During this time, I felt numb. I felt like a little bird lying half-stuck in the mud, my feathers were being slowly plucked out. Sometimes, it felt as if I would grow back a feather, only to have the one next to it get plucked. It was like one step forward, one step back. And I felt that way much of the time. I saw myself as that little bird who was lying in the mud in a cold, wet, naked, and vulnerable state.

Being around other people was emotionally exhausting for me, so I cut back on my shift work at the hospital and went to work for my cousin, who owned a nursery. Working with plants, flowers, and vegetables and basically playing in the dirt was more therapeutic than I could ever have imagined. The coworkers did not know me or nor did they ask any questions. I loved the anonymity of it all. I was only making seven dollars an hour, but there was no stress. It was a job I could handle in my fragile state.

Unfortunately, the job was available only during the main planting season and within a few months, I lost the safety net of earning money away from the pressures of everyday life. The pull to refocus on what I believe to be the murder of Pearl Justice became stronger as well, and I was increasingly frustrated by the lack of communication with the police. I was overcome with the guilt of not being able to remember that night for so long, and it didn't help that I was certain investigators and the County Attorney had written me off as some crazy old lady. The Sheriff at the time, Colin Lawson, wouldn't speak to me either.

Once again, I went to the County Attorney with some of my records that supported my belief that Pearl's death was murder, not an unfortunate accident. After our meeting, the County Attorney sent a letter to Sheriff Lawson informing him that I had important information regarding Pearl's case.

I waited patiently for a call from the Sheriff, but it never came. I called the County Attorney and requested a copy of the letter he had sent to Sheriff Lawson. I was curious about what he had said, but I also wanted to make sure a letter had in fact been sent. A few days later, the proof that a letter had indeed been sent to the Sheriff arrived in my mail.

I assumed the Sheriff would be interested in speaking with me about the new information in my possession, but that didn't seem to be the case. So, I placed a phone call to his office and asked to speak with him. I was placed on hold, but he never picked up my call. So, I called again on a different day, and once again the Sheriff never picked up my call. When I called a third time, Sheriff Lawson picked up the phone and hollered, "What do you want?"

I was rattled by his harshness, but managed to answer, "I want you to reopen the case of the murder of Pearl Justice."

"I'll get back to you later," he snapped. He then hung up on me. I never had the courage to call him again, and he never called me.

Eventually, I felt mentally and emotionally strong enough to return to hospital work but agreed to work only off-shifts because there were fewer people on duty. Stuttering had never been a problem in my life, but I found myself stuttering when I was talking to my supervisors or the doctors. To me, it was a sign that my self-confidence had hit rock bottom. Whenever I needed to report to work, I would cry all the way there. As soon as I got back into my truck to come home, I would cry all over again.

After December 22, 1993, I rarely felt safe in my own home. I had alarms placed on all of the doors, and there were times when I would be startled awake at night by the alarms, only to discover they had fallen to the floor due to the wind rattling the door. Finally, I had had enough of living in fear. That night I prayed to be awakened only if I needed to be awakened. Whatever the outcome of my life might be, I would surrender to Him and trust His will. Those words were calming enough for me to be able to take the bullet out of the chamber and put my rifle away for good.

During these anxious times, my kids were obviously concerned about me. It was a proud moment when I told them both that I was done living in fear and that whatever was to happen to me, I would accept it. I wrote a note on a piece of paper and put it in my file cabinet where they both could find it if I were ever to pass away.

> *Dear Sherry and William,*
> *I am just writing to tell you how much I love you. I really want to be able to spend time laughing, loving, and being with you. It can only come with peace in my life. I pray that God will still be guiding and watching over you as he has done so much in the past for me.*
> *Love, Mom*

Even though I was comforted by the grace of our Heavenly Father, I still struggled with talking about Pearl's death and gaining self-control over my thoughts and emotions. Every time I tried to talk about that night with someone in a position of authority, I would dissolve into tears. I was at a point of transition in my life and was still struggling to make sense of it all. I was also aware of how my pain made me appear to others. It has been shared with me over the years that people thought I was "weird."

As the months wore on, I still heard nothing from the investigating officer about Pearl's case. I dove headlong into gathering information about the case with the determination of an investigative reporter. I spent countless hours reading documents, forensic findings, lab reports, autopsy reports, and even viewed the photos from the burned kitchen that showed a melted clock that had stopped at 12:15 AM. I spent much of my spare time researching things like the flammable properties of car wax, medical terminology, and even police procedures.

There were plenty of facts that were accurate in the reports. Here are a few:

- Time of death was estimated to be in the range of 11:30 PM to 12:30 AM.
- Her body was found face down with her head pressing against the kitchen cupboard. Her glasses were broken and laying in close proximity to her body.
- The exterior of the house showed no physical damage from the fire. Interior smoke damage was limited to a small area around the kitchen window, which was cracked open slightly. *"It appeared the window had been open prior to the fire."* The outside temp that night was 25 below zero. There was no reason for the window to be open.
- The scene report stated that the area of the fire was contained to an area around her body and the fronts of the kitchen cupboards. It was also noted that the fire had burned "hot and fast" and there were candles across the room that were melted, but not destroyed.
- The first deputy on the scene noted several burned matchsticks on the counter, and an accelerant substance was noted on the areas around the body and the adjacent carpeting.

- The Supplementary Police Report noted that a family member had dropped Pearl off at her home the evening of December 21 around 8:30 PM, after they had attended a family function. Pearl was in good spirits and good health at the time.
- As to the condition of her body, it was noted that her nightgown and robe had burned away.
- When the Fire Department arrived around 8:30 AM that morning, there were no flames or remnants of smoke in the air.

As I read and researched, I documented dozens of inconsistencies and unanswered questions, including:

- Pearl's death was listed as *"undetermined cardiac arrest."*
- The autopsy also revealed that there were gray cloth fibers in her throat, same color and type as the chair cushions in the kitchen.
- The police report assumed that the fire department broke the lock on Pearl's door to gain entry, yet the delivery man who discovered her body and called 911 stated he opened the door and looked inside.
- The police reports identified the large black garbage bag filled with papers sitting just outside of the fire-damaged kitchen. Upon sifting through the papers, they found many of Pearl's personal documents, like her husband's death certificate and tax records. They were things that she would not have destroyed or thrown out. The Fire Marshal also noted that there was liquid residue on the papers that smelled of paint thinner or mineral spirits. Pearl's family couldn't explain the chemical-soaked bag of important documents either.
- Being from an older generation, Pearl was in the habit of keeping a can of grease on her stovetop. It's an old-school

habit to which many young people cannot relate. Since this was part of her everyday life, she would not have put the grease can ON a burner. Yet, a can of "bubbling" grease was present on a burner when the fire department arrived.

- Crime scene documentation and photos revealed a wad of a fabric softener sheet tied on the doorknob going downstairs to Pearl's basement. It was noted that it had been placed there before the fire and had melted onto the doorknob. Pearl never went down to her basement because of her arthritic knees. This would have only been placed on the doorknob if someone was trying to avoid leaving fingerprints.

- There was a sooty, smeared handprint on the counter, blisters on her hands, and fresh scratches on the counter near Pearl's body, all indicating she was still conscious and trying to break her fall when she went down.

- The original report noted there were "smudges" in the soot surrounding her body. This was later amended to note that they were footmarks of the first fireman on the scene.

- The first fireman who walked into the kitchen picked up the smoldering chair cushion and threw it out the door. I believe this cushion was actually used to end Pearl's life after she fell to the ground from the blow to her head. The cushion was then used to smother her. I believe one of the men held her down by the back of her neck and pushed her face into the cushion. Unable to breathe, she may have gone into cardiac arrest, but she also could have died from suffocation. Unfortunately, we will never know because the tossed cushion was never retrieved or logged as evidence. Crime scene photos showed it laying on the deck under a table and in the snow.

- The Sheriff's officer, who was first on the scene that day, noted in his report that there was a significant amount of blood spatter on the cupboard doors near the body.

This officer also noted that there was blood spatter on the underside of the countertop lip, remarking on how odd it was that blood would splash up to that point.

- Samples from the scene were taken and sent for testing. When the tests came back, they showed high levels of petroleum distillate, and no grease. Mineral oil, naphtha, heavy fuel oil, waxes, and benzene are examples of petroleum distillates. In my mind, the lab tests confirmed that grease from the stove was *not* the accelerant.

- It had always been my belief that the two men at Pearl's that night used car wax as an accelerant, since it's highly flammable. I believe that, when it was discovered the next day that one of the stove burners was on, it was turned on by one of the intruders. The wax I had researched had a low flashpoint (170 degrees) and its fast ignition process would have given the murderers only seconds to escape before it exploded.

- The Fire Marshal also noted that the covers on Pearl's bed were thrown back as if she was in bed, but then got out of it. Knowing her as I did, I knew it was out of character for my elderly friend to be up late at night. His scenario:

It is in my opinion that this fire was accidental in nature. While waiting for the items in the oven to finish baking, the victim went to bed to read a book. While reading, she became aware of a problem in the kitchen. Upon her investigation, she discovered a can of grease bubbling on the stovetop. While trying to remove the can, she caught her clothing on fire. She suffered a heart attack while trying to extinguish the fire. I was misinformed by Deputy Al Lang that the cause of death was a heart attack, and the carbon Monoxide level was at 4%. And the patient died from Cardiac arrest.

- An investigating deputy who attended the autopsy overheard the coroner state that Pearl had died of "undetermined cardiac arrest," and mistakenly assumed that cardiac arrest was the same as a heart attack. That incorrect information was shared with other agencies involved in Pearl's case. Based on that comment, there was no more investigative work to be done and no investigators went door to door and asked questions.

To say that I became "fully immersed" in Pearl's story may be an understatement. As my focus became more intense on shifting this case from "closed" to "active," parts of my life were neglected, including my attention to my two adult children. Sherry would get so angry with me when she would stop by and see me researching something related to the case. "*MOM, Let It GO!*" she would scream. "Why do you have one drama after another? You have never been here for us!"

And she was right. I wasn't there for my family. Because of my profound emotional pain, I had simply checked out on everything.

I believe in my heart that Pearl did not suffer the night she died. The autopsy stated there was evidence of a blow to the head and there was no smoke in her lungs. So, it was a safe bet that she was dead before the kitchen was set on fire. As for the missing jewelry, no one will ever know.

The investigating deputy, Al Lang, ultimately admitted to Pearl's daughter-in-law that "Something happened here, and I don't know what it is. The only one who truly knows is Pearl, and she's not talking."

Chapter 12

Attorneys Sold My Property

NOW KNOWING THAT THE TWO MEN he had sent to my house to retrieve all the attorney's files were unsuccessful, Ed resurfaced and decided he would illegally sell my property and businesses out from under me. By the ruling of the courts, Ed was managing the car wash business and leasing it from me. The monthly income from this lease agreement was helping me pay my bills and keep my farm afloat.

Proud and arrogant, Ed never let on that I was the true owner of the business and told everyone that he was. So, my ex-husband sold my property and business to a man named Howard Forrester. Not long after, I received a phone call from a nurse friend who I formerly worked with in southern Minnesota. She informed me that my car wash was for sale and Caldwell Bankers had the listing. She gave me the phone number of the real estate office and I quickly made a call to the realtor, Mr. Bly. When I asked the realtor if my Full-Service Car Wash was for sale, he confirmed that it was.

I asked him, "How can you sell a business without the owner knowing?" I angrily challenged him. "I am 50 percent owner of the car wash and the land it sits on, and I have no intention of selling it!"After our phone call he immediately sent out a letter. Here is an excerpt:

> *"As you are all aware, there is a dispute between the parties of this agreement as to whether or not this is a valid contract. Please be advised that the Caldwell Banker/ at your service realty, LTD is in receipt of a $5,000.00 earnest money check written by Howard Forrester and made payable to our trust account. We have been advised to hold this check and not deposit it into our account until all parties (both buyers and sellers) agree as to its disposition.*
>
> *We hope this matter can be resolved to the satisfaction of all parties. We will await your collective agreement before we proceed."*

He then revealed to me that on 7/20/94 he and my attorney, Ross Irwin, had a meeting with Ed's new attorney and during it, the buyers attempted to back out of the sale. All of this occurred without my knowledge or permission. Mr. Bly also shared that on 7/22/94, he had sent out a letter to the addresses of myself, Ed Klein, Roger Hammer, and Howard Forrester. No such letter had ever made it to me.

The potential new buyer, Howard Forrester, had backed out of the sale, and Ed (who owned no part of the business) took him to court for Breach of Contract. The judge at the proceedings, Judge Mett, ruled that the signature of Jeanie Hall (me) was necessary for the sale of this property.

On 8/5/94, my attorney had a conference with Robert Fredrickson, the broker for the car wash. Ed, along with his crony, Max Walker, decided they were going to do what they needed to do to get the ownership of the car wash and property away from me. In the fall of 1995, my attorney met with Ed and his new wife Marge, along with Max Walker, to discuss selling my property. Again, this was all done without my knowledge or consent.

Unbeknownst to me, my attorney was actively attempting to sell the property deeded to me in the divorce decree, the Full-Service Car Wash. It was my sole possession. And I was not about to lose it without a fight. The thought of losing my monthly lease payments, thanks to more of my ex-husband's underhanded shenanigans, made my blood run cold.

My attorney, without my knowledge or consent, then drew up a lease which stated that Max Walker could lease the car wash and property with the option to purchase the land and the business.

Max eventually sent me a formal letter of his intentions and I answered that I had no intention of selling my property. He began sending me my monthly lease payments, which helped me financially. It appears he was sending me my payments as a sign of good faith, but it was likely more for manipulative reasons. I accepted his checks under the belief that he was sending the money because he was acting as a new partner with Ed. I had signed nothing, including a lease, and I hoped the money would continue coming so I could make my farm payments.

Max sent me a total of five lease checks before sending me a formal letter stating that he was going to exercise his right to purchase my property. Again, I informed him via letter that my property was not for sale. On November 3, 1995, my attorney sent a letter to Ed and Marge Klein, Roger Hammer, and Max Walker informing them that he no longer represented me.

On December 1, 1995, my former attorney met with Max and typed up a Real Estate Purchase Agreement that stated my signature was not required. Once again, I knew nothing about what my former attorney was doing behind my back.

To top things off, my now former attorney, Ross Irwin, sued me for a total of $42,853.06 and sent all documentation three different ways, via the police department, by certified mail, and by regular postal service. Within a two-week period, I sent him two letters in response that acknowledged the receipt of this information. Ultimately, he told the courts that he "never heard anything from me." As a result, on December 15, 1995, he obtained a judgment against me. He then proceeded to garnish my lease payments from the car wash.

When my attorney dropped me as a client and sued me, he printed out on his computer all the bills under my name. Included in those bills were some that had already been paid but were still active in his computer. Also included were bills generated for the "Sale of Car Wash" and his meetings with my ex-husband and his wife and Max. This was my first knowledge of a conflict of interest my attorney was creating.

As I stared at an attorney bill that was filled with charges for things I never approved, I had to wonder what power Ed had over my attorney to get him to drop me and start working for him. Ross never billed Ed for the things that were clearly requested by him and charged the fees to my account instead.

Since my attorney's secretary had mistakenly given me the incriminating illegal records, I can only surmise that my attorney had asked Ed to get the records back. If so, does this make my former attorney an accessory to the murder? Or did my attorney fall victim to Ed's control?

In December of 1996, Ross Irwin sold the car wash, the only asset that I received in my divorce, to Max Walker. I was unaware of the sale, but I asked my nurse friend to go to the courthouse and see if the property was still in my name. She reported back to me that it was.

Without my lease payments, I was breaking and struggling financially. I made the bold decision to represent myself in court and told my former attorney this fact. I requested a jury trial and was sent the forms. I now needed time to prepare mentally and emotionally for yet another fight. I met a lovely lady at work who happened to be married to a retired attorney. I told her my former attorney had dropped me as a client and sued me for the balance of his fees from representing me in my divorce. I was representing myself against a major law firm in Minneapolis.

She and her husband lived on Diamond Lake, which was not far from my farm. After I confided in her about my legal battle, she informed her husband, Ken Greenfield, that he needed to swing by my house and talk to me immediately. When they stopped by one evening, my dining room was covered in legal documents and files. Ken had been a pro bono attorney and had always enjoyed helping clients who were in tough situations, like me.

Together, we sent my attorney interrogatories that included hard questions like:

- Did you diligently represent me?
- Did you efficiently represent me?
- Did you conscientiously represent me?
- Have your invoices been honest, truthful, and accurate?

Thankfully, I had plenty of time to prepare for court, but it felt like an eternity before my court date finally arrived. At last, I could state my case in front of a judge. I took the month of April 1998 off from work to prepare fully for my court appearance. Ken had given me volumes of records to memorize so I would conduct myself as a competent and professional defendant. Finally, April 28,1998 arrived, and I asked my cousin Amber to make the three-hour drive to the Sanford County Courthouse and support me during the proceedings as well.

Amber and I were waiting outside the courtroom when Ross walked up to where we were sitting. He said to me, "There will be no jury trial. I'll get this dismissed without prejudice and see to it that you never get your money." That comment only made me angrier and more determined to demand justice.

Once in the courtroom, I was the first to speak directly to the judge. I told him, "Your Honor, this man has sued me for money that I do not owe him. I also know he does not report all of his income to his law firm."

Ross immediately jumped to his feet and hollered, "Strike

that!" The Judge then requested that the two of us try to resolve our differences and asked everyone but Ross, Amber and myself to leave the courtroom. When the room was empty, I turned to Ross and asked him point-blank why he dropped me as a client, then sued me.

"I was trying to help you," he replied.

"HELP me? You took away my lease payments and I am about to lose my farm. How is that helping me?"

At that moment, Ross realized that the microphone on our table was on, and he quickly switched it off. Then the Judge came back into the room and asked, "Did you two reach an agreement?" We responded that we had.

Our agreement involved a settlement for me to pay $5,000 for the judgment, only after Ross, my attorney, collected $15,000 from my ex-husband, as ordered by the Judge. The Judge also ordered Ross to do what was needed to get the car wash and property returned to me. Ross never disclosed to the Judge or to me, that my property was taken away from me by Eminent Domain a year earlier.

The downside is that there was an Eminent Domain motion filed in September 1997 before I ever found out about it. Basically, Eminent Domain is the right of a government or its agent to expropriate private property for public use, with payment of compensation. An attorney representing the buyer sent a letter to the city attorney that he would notify the property owners. He never notified me. The attorney, head of the commission (which has a membership of four who are to not know or to have any contact with the property owners), transferred my mortgage on the car wash from First Bank in Minneapolis to Max Walker.

When we found out about the Eminent Domain, my new attorney, Ken, came out of retirement and sued the new buyers in court for the illegal sale of my property. The buyers knew that the property was a partnership and had requested that my partner, Roger, not respond to the condemnation and that I not be notified of it. They knew the sale was in violation of the partnership agreement. See statute 323.08 and 323.09.

STATUTE 323.08 AND 323.09

323.08

States there part of the UPA or Uniform Partnership Act, those stated say that if there is a restriction in the Partnership Agreement a buyer who buys from a partner, who violates the restriction cannot have title, if he knows about the restriction.

323.09

A buyer from that buyer who also knows about the restriction cannot get title and .09 says that the partnership can have the property back.

Roger Hammer was brought to court in shackles to testify after being convicted of sexually molesting his stepdaughters. It was quite a sight to see him come into court escorted by a policeman, with cuffs on his hands and feet and the big chain around his waist connecting both.

In court, Roger lied and stated he was never my partner, he was only Ed's. Unfortunately for him, there were countless documents proving that he was indeed my business partner. There were so many unpaid bills, property taxes, attorney's fees, liens and expenses that there was little money remaining from the sale. On September 15, 1997, title to my property was transferred to Max Walker, who immediately signed it over to the new buyers.

After all was done, I sent my packet of records to an attorney who specialized in Eminent Domains. He returned my records telling me that he could prove that I owned the property, but the City Attorney would never take it away from the new owners and give it back to me. He informed me that I would just end up with additional attorney fees.

He said, "You have to bite the bullet."

Chapter 13

Homeless

My divorce may have been finalized, but my troubles were far from over. Endless problems, court fees, and attorney's costs left me broke and broken.

My saving grace was that I was able to continue my nursing work at the hospital in a neighboring town, and the income helped a little. But since I was no longer receiving my lease payments from the Full-Service Car Wash, I was unable to make my farm payments. I could only wait until the farm was foreclosed on from not making the payments.

After my being delinquent on farm payments for a year, my beloved farm was sold to satisfy my debt. This left me with nothing but my personal possessions, a beat-up truck, and my horses. I had no place to live and couldn't afford to rent a house. Thankfully, my daughter and her husband and my son and his wife came home to help me move. Since I had nowhere to live, my household items were put in storage, and I had to rent pasture space so my horses would have a place to go.

For a while, I lived in a room I rented from my uncle in town. It was better than nothing, but it really bothered me that my kids had no place to come to visit me. Every morning I would drive out of town where my horses were pastured and check on them and feed them. For almost four months in the summer, I lived in an old pop-up trailer that was held together by duct tape. The trailer was parked on a friend's land, and I had no running water or electricity. My "shower" consisted of my bathing in the lake every morning. My only source of power to keep my phone charged was the charger inside my vehicle.

Every morning after doing my chores, I would walk over to the nearby resort and give riding lessons on Shetland ponies to the children of the resort guests. After saddling the pony and helping the riders get on, I would walk beside them and teach them about horse care and behaviors as we walked through the woods.

Once they were comfortable on their mounts, the children were taught how to turn and how to stop their horses. It was a peaceful existence, and I loved teaching the next generation how to be riders. One proud mom even confided to me that her daughter told her that I had taught her everything she needed to know about horses. It made my day!

Even though my living situation was sparse and humble, I felt safe and comfortable living in my camper on an island. It was a simple way of life that I sometimes miss even now.

Occasionally, my friends would feel sorry for me and my rough living conditions. I would always respond that they didn't know it, but my little camper was parked in a place I referred to as Paradise Island. Everyone should be so lucky! Eventually, I was able to rent a house and keep a couple of my horses there. As part of my rental agreement, I was responsible for taking care of my landlord's horses, and I didn't mind at all.

I was so happy to have a place to live.

Chapter 14

The Coroner's Inquest of 2001

In January 2000, my attorney, Ken, contacted the Sparrow County Attorney's Office with my concerns and now recollected memories about Pearl's death. I could not simply sit on the sidelines without being heard fully one last time.

The County Attorney, Shaw Mayfield, met with Ken and was in turn referred to Dr. Shannon Camp, the Sparrow County Coroner. The information was reviewed, and following a consultation with the County Attorney, the Sparrow County Coroner decided to convene an inquest.

The Presiding Officer at the inquest was Hennepin County Medical Examiner, Dr. Clark Remford, who was appointed by the Assistant Sparrow County Coroner *pro hac vice* for this purpose. For those who are unsure of what an inquest is (and its purpose), I can share this:

> *An inquest is a public court hearing held by the coro-*
> *ner to establish who died and how, when and where the*
> *death occurred. Consideration of 'how' a person died is*

generally understood to mean "by what means and in what circumstances".

Part one of the inquest initially convened in the first part of May 2001 at the Sparrow County Courthouse. This inquest was the first of its kind to take place in Minnesota, so it was obviously unfamiliar territory for all involved. Also subpoenaed was the Fire Marshal, Deputy Lang, and me.

Things didn't go well from the start:

- Much time was spent trying to cast doubt on why there were petechial hemorrhages in Pearl's eyes.
- Even though I was subpoenaed to testify as a witness, there is no record of any of my testimony.
- Dr. Remford and Dr. Camp testified that they went to my residence, stood in my driveway, and stated that they *"could not clearly see the deceased's home"* even though I had stated I was in the horse pen **behind** Pearl's house. They even mocked me and joked that I *"must have used an extension ladder or binoculars."*

Although it was springtime and there was more foliage than there would have been when the decedent died in the winter, it was clear from the inspection that the witness's (my) recollection was neither plausible or possible.

- It was reported that my memory of that night took four years to return even though I had made it abundantly clear that it had returned five months after the incident at Pearl's.
- After the lengthy explanation of Ed's criminal ties and intentions, and the timeline that supported my belief that he was responsible directly or indirectly for Pearl's death, no one believed me.

In July 2001, part two of the inquest took place, this time at the Helland County Medical Examiner's office in the Metro in order to take the testimony of their acting Medical Examiner, James Sand. The doctor confirmed all the autopsy findings and discounted any significant physical injury other than thermal injury. He stated that the petechial hemorrhage in the sclera of Pearl's eyes and the blood staining on the back of her neck were *artifactual*. Upon looking up "artifactual" in Webster's Dictionary, I found the word is described… as *being any object made by human work*.

In between court dates, I dug a little deeper into what happens when petechial hemorrhaging forms in the eyes of a deceased person. An online information site shared that petechial hemorrhaging is a form of mild hemorrhage which has distinctive markings known as petechiae. The condition emerges when the capillaries near the surface of the body burst. When people are asphyxiated, a classical petechial hemorrhage develops in their eyes as the blood vessels burst. This can also occur by strangulation, suffocation, or by hanging. This hemorrhaging would not have been present in Pearl's eyes for no reason.

Despite that inconsistency, the coroner stood by his autopsy findings that stated the subject's death was due to *fatal cardiac arrhythmia due to thermal injuries; injuries suffered while in her private residence.* This was an upgrade from "undetermined cardiac arrest," but still not accurate in my eyes. The manner of death was ruled as accidental.

The death of Pearl Justice involved several departments in the investigation after her body was found in her home following a fire on December 22, 1993. As a result of the death investigation, a death certificate was filed listing the manner of death as accidental and the cause of death was probably a fatal cardiac arrhythmia resulting from thermal injuries. Housefire was listed in the section of how the injury occurred.

> *The complainant's testimony is lengthy and com-*
> *plex and requires substantial background explanation*
> *as part of the questioning. The delivery and narrative*
> *of her testimony were fundamentally persuasive. After*
> *careful scrutiny, however, it is concluded that her testi-*
> *mony contains numerous details strongly inconsistent*
> *with the death scene investigation and autopsy findings.*
> *Dr. Camp and Dr. Remford did not find her testimony*
> *to be credible.*

The finality and harshness of the words on the page made my heart sink to my toes. Once again, I felt completely unheard. But I wasn't about to give up . . . yet.

In November 2001, I wrote a letter to the Sparrow County Attorney expressing my displeasure at the outcome of the Coroner's Inquest. I asked for an appeal of the inquest findings based on these truths and missteps:

1. I felt it was crucial to have an accurate sight inspection of the witness (me). What I witnessed that night could not be viewed from the road or even from my driveway, since it is at least 300 feet from where I was actually standing the night of December 22, 1993.

2. Contrary to what Deputy Lang testified, my memory of that night did not return four years later. It was between five and six months after her death that my traumatic amnesia lifted enough for me to recall clearly what I saw that night at Pearl's.

3. Dr. Sand stated during the inquest that the petechial hemorrhages described in the sclera of the eyes, and the blood staining on the back of Pearl's neck, were the result of disease or injury. In his report, the following paragraph then stated that the deceased died while trying to put out the fire. This sounded like a contradiction to me, and I stated

that in my letter. Petechial hemorrhages can be caused from extreme prostration and could have been the result of an intruder's attack.

4. I testified that I heard arguing in the house that night and that one of the voices was Pearl's. If she was conscious when the fire started and was burned, I would have heard her screams.

5. The can of grease on the stove was blamed as the fire accelerant, yet the test from the lab reported only traces of a petroleum distillate substance that was **not** animal fat from cooking grease.

6. During the inquest, Dr. Sand noted the scuff marks in the soot around the body and determined that Pearl was alive when the fire occurred. When in fact, the first fireman on the scene reported he walked in, passed the body, picked up the smoldering cushion to throw outside, and walked past the body again. The "scuff marks" in the soot were likely from the fireman's boots.

7. Dr. Sand also claimed that Pearl was alive when the fire erupted in her home, yet the low levels of carbon monoxide in her lungs that were noted during her autopsy proved otherwise.

8. Because law enforcement immediately assumed that Pearl's death was an accident, no interviews of neighbors or door-to-door canvassing was done.

I ended my letter with these words:

I feel as though I am entitled to express my displeasure at your failure to respond to my repeated telephone calls. In fact, my attorney told me that he had left a call recently as well that has gone unanswered. I also know that, at your suggestion, my attorney sent an in-depth and detailed report of what I witnessed that night and that I am certain that what I saw was the homicide of Pearl Justice.

Realistically, I am aware that my demands cannot be a welcomed addition to your workload. I can assure you that what I witnessed the night of December 22, 1993, was not welcomed by me either. Nonetheless, I saw two men leaving the house at the exact time of the victim's death. These recollections will not go away, and neither will I.

I am a registered nurse and I have more than enough medical experience to know that the existing autopsy report was an evasion of responsibility. There is no statute of limitations on homicides; nor on the responsibility of those tasked with duties related to homicide.

So, with respect, I implore you to have a telephone conversation or a meeting with me. I am ready to be tested by cross-examination or polygraph.

Ten days later I received a response from his office:

I am in receipt of, and have reviewed, your letter and am also in receipt of the final Order arising out of the Coroner's Inquest surrounding Ms. Justice's death. From the tone of your letter, it is my impression that you disagree with the Coroner's Inquest result. However, I consider this matter concluded and have consequently closed my file. Therefore, the Sparrow County Attorney's office will have no further involvement in this matter.

Once again, the door to any hope of justice for Pearl slammed shut. Head down and discouraged, I moved forward with my life, but my friend was never far from my mind.

Chapter 15

I Bought a Farm

In 2004, I was finally on the road to recovering from my difficult financial struggles. I was working steadily, and my bills were being paid on time. Soon, I found a 20-acre farm with a beautiful and relatively new barn. The barn had four box stalls, a lounge, a tack room, and a grain room. In the center of the barn was a round pen that could be perfect for exercising and training my horses. I fell in love with the barn and knew I would work with my horses there and build a new life.

The house was older than the barn, but it was a diamond in the rough. It had three bedrooms and two bathrooms, and I did as much remodeling on it as I could afford. Best of all, my kids now had a place where they could come home. During these years, my daughter and her husband blessed me with a granddaughter, and they lived just two miles away from my farm. My son and his wife had also blessed me with a grandson and granddaughter, and they lived 4 1/2 hours away. It was such a relief for me that both of my children now had a place they could come home to. It seemed like things were finally starting to shift in my favor.

I could only pay $5,000 down on the farm, so my monthly mortgage payments were quite high. I remained on a very tight budget because I was determined not to lose this property as well. On my first spring on the farm, I bred nine mares, hoping to get at least six foals. But in the spring of 2006, I was blessed with **nine** little darlings! Abundance was beginning to flow to me once again.

That spring was a busy one, with many pregnant mares and many little foals to watch after. On top of it all, I was working the late shift at the hospital. Many nights I would get home at midnight, only to change clothes and hurry to the barn to prepare for the delivery of yet another baby. Luckily, since my daughter lived close, she would come down in the mornings and help me out by cleaning some of the stalls.

One evening, while I was at work, one of my mares went into labor. My sister was doing a barn check, and she called me and told me about the laboring mare. My daughter and her husband immediately came to help my sister and over the phone, I was able to coach them and give them instructions on how to bring this new life into the world. It was a complicated delivery because the placenta had become detached. It took all three of them to pull the foal out. Miraculously, both the baby and mom survived. They named the filly, Jellybean, because they were all eating jellybeans while waiting for the delivery.

Around this time, since I had two beautiful stallions, I began dabbling in breeding mares from other owners. The first stallion I had raised myself, and the second was a gift from someone who just wanted him to have a good home. I felt fortunate to be his owner because not only was he a beautiful black stallion, but he was also a racehorse that had run in the Belmont Stakes in 2000.

With my children raised and most of my worries with Ed over, my horses were my passion, and they brought me joy in many ways.

Chapter 16

My Four-Legged Children

DURING THE TIME I WAS SLOGGING THROUGH the nightmare that was my divorce proceedings, there were three main things that kept me sane.

The first was my two adult children. During these dark years, they continued to be sources of light in my life and gave me a comforting shoulder to lean on whenever they could.

The second was my nursing career, because it gave me a sense of purpose and caring for others seemed to fill the hollow spots in my heart. There were many days between 1986 and 1993 when I was so mentally and emotionally drained that I didn't want to go to work. But once I was there, the joy that I received from helping others and making their day special kept me from descending completely into darkness. I was very thankful for the distraction that was my work.

The third sanity-saver was my horses. My love for horses began when I was a child in my hometown of North Town and, as an adult, horses were always part of my life. I had over a dozen thoroughbreds on my farm, and they were (and still are) like four-legged angels with fur and hooves. Just taking care of them and meeting their needs kept my day full. Their soulful eyes and feisty energy greeted me every morning and welcomed me home every night.

By 2004, I had settled into life at my new farm in North Town. Between family, work, and my horses, my days were busy. Most days I would collapse onto my couch at 6:30 PM. I was exhausted from all the work and my busy schedule, but my constant responsibilities helped me sleep soundly at night. It also gave me a sense of pride during a time when I was feeling lost and beat down. The accomplishment and satisfaction from knowing how much work I had completed in a day was what kept me motivated to get up the next day and do it all over again.

It was during these years that I became very interested in raising and racing thoroughbreds. I found great joy in being a horse breeder and trainer. Sitting in the grandstands at what is now known as Canterbury Park, watching the horse that I raised from a foal race down a track toward the finish line was (and still is) one of the biggest highs in my life. Watching my beautiful racehorses come prancing out on the track always filled my eyes with tears. I was like a proud mama.

All my horses were raised with respect and love and not once did a horse give me trouble. It is amazing to me how horses can communicate with you. They are so intuitive. So wise. So intelligent. They can sense when you're upset, and their behavior will also tell when they are upset.

But the one facet of raising and training horses that I loved more than anything was helping to bring new babies into the world. Every spring, I would have babies to deliver. A mare's gestation period is around 345 days and a veterinarian once told me that the only thing you can count on with a pregnant mom is that she will repeat her birthing pattern. I'll never forget the time one of my mares acted as if she was going to deliver a day early and I was puzzled that she was not staying true to her birthing pattern. Then

I realized it was a leap year and there was one extra day I had not accounted for!

My dedication to my horses included spending nights sleeping on straw in my barn to make sure everyone came through the birth process safely. This habit also helped me save foals that otherwise might have died. Sometimes the birth experience is so traumatic that the babies have trouble standing and finding their mommies. It's critical that they stand and feed on their own within the first few hours of birth.

When a foal made its first appearance, it was a magical moment when all my cares and worries washed away. The thrill of watching a brand-new life stand up, work its way to its mommy, and witnessing them "talk" to each other is hard to put into words. I never minded missing sleep just to make sure mom and baby were fine.

Raising young horses takes a lot of hard work, patience, and perseverance. I was able to observe and learn from some of the top experts in the horse training business. I also worked with and shadowed farriers over the years as well. A farrier is a specialist in equine hoof care, including the trimming and balancing of horses' hooves and the placing of shoes on their hooves, if necessary. Hoof-care and proper shoeing are critical to the success of racehorses. It was a busy and exhilarating project and there were many times when I used vacation days from my hospital work to be at the track when my three-year-old racehorses ran races.

Despite all the joy my horses brought me, there were sad times, too. One year one of my mares passed away during the birthing process and I was devastated. Her baby was a beautiful boy with four white socks and a big star on his head. Because his mama had passed, I became his surrogate mama and he bonded to me quickly. I used a milk replacer to feed him, and this little colt could eat like a big boy and guzzle down two bottles without stopping.

Just as with human babies, I needed to go out and feed my little man every two hours. I started buying goat's milk for him and he grew big and strong from my love and care. He was also quite shy and oftentimes he hung close to me when we joined the other horses outside. I would also let him suck on my thumb or finger whenever he would get stressed. It wasn't long before he was drinking from a bucket, and I stretched out his feeding schedule.

Unfortunately, tragedy struck in the most unusual of ways. One day I let him out of the barn while I was cleaning his pen, which was our normal routine. Off in the distance I saw lightning, but it was miles away and I felt I had time to finish his pen before the storm hit. But it was only a matter of minutes into cleaning the pen when I heard a loud bang. Frantically, I ran out to see what happened. Lightning had struck the barn and my baby was dead. Even though it was a freak accident, I cried and cried, and it took years for me to forgive myself.

When you raise animals, you know that the circle of life is part of the process. With life, comes death. But, at the time, it was just one more blow to my already fragile emotions.

Chapter 17

One Last Call and
My Darkest Days

JUST AS LIFE WAS GETTING BRIGHTER, tragedy struck again.

On March 5, 2007, my only son, William, was killed when a teenage girl driving a truck, decided to run a stop sign causing a collision. He was killed instantly, and she survived the accident. He was only 39 years old and would have turned 40 in two months. My daughter, Sherry and I received a call from William's wife, who informed us of the accident and that it was fatal. We were devastated that we never got to say goodbye.

My son was loved by everyone. He had a kind heart and was the best son a mother could ever ask for. He was a wonderful husband, father, and brother, too. Having him taken from us so soon was heartbreaking. Knowing he was with God gave me some comfort, but I missed him so much.

My daughter was inconsolable and worried that William died not knowing how much she loved him. My depression and anxiety returned. Daily I prayed to God and my son in heaven to help me through the day. The church that held his funeral was packed with his friends, his family, coworkers, teachers, and the dozens of people whose lives had been touched by his warmth and kindness. There was a lot of snow on the ground even though it was March, not an uncommon occurrence in Minnesota. On the day of the funeral, the sun shone brightly in a clear sky. The warmth from it radiated all around us, melting the snow and comforting us. The depth of my sadness at the loss of my son was almost too much to bear.

After the service was over, my nephew, Gus, shared with me that he had stopped at the crash site on his way to the funeral. As he stood at the site where my son left this earth, he looked down and saw William's watch and his cellphone. The sun had melted the snow just enough for him to find these things. I truly believe that Gus was at the right place at the right time and that my son's guardian angels knew he needed to find those items. Teary-eyed, Gus quietly placed the watch and cell phone into my shaking hands. I was overcome with grief, and at the same time, incredibly moved to be able to hold these pieces of my son.

As the days turned to weeks, I would often call William's cell phone just so I could hear his voice again. The phone was dead from the crash and being left in the elements, so I was unable to turn it on. But when I would call his number, it gave me great comfort to hear William's voice-recorded message.

Two weeks after the funeral, I was awakened at around 2:15 AM by the sound of soft music. I lay in my bed, listened intently, and tried to isolate where it was coming from. The sounds were soft and pleasant, yet it seemed so far away that I could barely hear it. The music would briefly get louder before fading away again. It took me a few moments to realize that the sound must be a cell phone ring even though I knew it wasn't my ringtone. And it almost sounded as if it was coming from outside my house.

Driven by curiosity, I jumped out of bed and went to the window to look outside. The early morning was quiet and calm and there was clearly no one there. I went to the kitchen and heard the music again. It was louder this time.

That's when I saw it.

Lying in the middle of the table next to my phone was William's cellphone, but it wasn't dead. It was lit up and flashing. Mesmerized, I picked it up, but I didn't push any buttons. I had no clue how to work his phone, so I could only speculate that it was doing an update or had somehow magically recharged. As I held it in my hand, the soft music suddenly stopped.

Then, as clearly as if he were standing next to me, I heard, *"Hi Mom, it's William. I want you to know that I am OK, and everything is fine."*

I sobbed with joy. He sounded so good. My son was OK! I wanted to call my daughter and give her the news, but it was 2:30 AM. She was a new mom with a two-month-old baby, so sleep was priceless. I went to bed with comfort in my heart. I called Sherry around 8:00 AM and told her the beautiful story of how William had called me in the night.

She listened to me quietly, and when I was done, she said, *"Mom, William came to me last night, too."*

As she lay sleeping, she woke suddenly to see her brother standing by her closed bedroom door. In those moments, she was able to tell him how much she loved him and missed him. She then told me that, when his form disappeared, a piece of her heart went with him. I asked her, *"How did he look?"*

Sherry replied, *"Mom, he looked just great."*

My beloved son knew that I needed to know that he was OK, and his sister needed to be able to tell him one last time how much she loved him. It was the greatest gift that I could have ever asked for. The next day we were both still flying high from the memory of that beautiful visit. But when I called William's phone to hear his voice one last time, I received the message that the phone number was no longer in service. That visit was his final goodbye and an assurance that we would all be just fine.

Later that spring, an acquaintance stopped by my house with her two grandchildren. She wanted to show them my new baby foals. As the children played, she turned to me and said, "You lost your son, yes?"

I nodded, but my intuition instantly told me that she had suffered the same loss. I said, "So did you."

I then told her about my phone call from my son in heaven. When I got to the part about the flashing of the ringing phone on my table, she interrupted me and said, "He called you to tell you he was OK, right?"

I responded, *"Yes"*, but also asked how she knew that. She replied that her son gifted her with that same message on the day of his funeral. The message was, *"Mom, I'm OK."*

I knew right then and there that I was going to rise up from this new pain and be even stronger than ever, someday.

Chapter 18

The Murder
Investigation Continues

IT WAS NOW 2015 AND, EVEN AFTER all the trauma and injustices in my life, I was able to move on. With one exception. The murder of my neighbor still haunted me. A dear friend who lived close by offered to spend time with me to help me get this story on paper. It was (and still is) my hope that this process will be a psychological relief for me, and I can finally heal and move on.

In the spring of 2016, we decided to go to the County Court Administrator Building where the inquest had been held. We were looking for any additional information on Pearl's death. The building is high security, so those wanting to enter need to call from the entrance, state their purpose for being there, and then go through another layer of security which includes having your possessions searched and walking through a body scanner.

Once we were inside, the clerk behind the desk was very helpful and located some new information for us. I already had all the documentation surrounding the inquest in my possession, but much to our surprise, we were presented details about an inquest that had been held in the Twin Cities without my knowledge. There were 27 pages of notes, and the inquest involved the coroner who conducted Pearl's autopsy back in 1993.

These documents stated that over 45 pictures and some video taken of the original crime scene were included in the second Inquest, but when I asked to see them, the clerk said she was unable to find them. I paid her $10 for copies of the new information that she did have and took them home. Armed with new details, my friend and I had renewed determination to investigate further the death of Pearl Justice.

On April 18, 2016, I wrote a letter to the County Attorney asking for assistance in finding the missing pictures from the second inquest. On June 2, 2016, we attended a meeting with the County Attorney. As I retold my story of that night once again, he repeatedly interjected, "You believe" as I relayed the details of what I had seen at Pearl's the night she died.

"You believe" soon got very annoying, and I shot back, "No, I don't *'believe'* . . . I *know*!" I showed him a copy of the 911 call that was made by the Schwan's delivery man and that included details of how he "opened the door and looked inside." This directly conflicted with the statement that Pearl's door "had to be damaged by arriving rescuers to gain entry." Then I informed him that I had made a phone call to the first fireman on the scene at Pearl's house. I had some questions for him that he willingly answered. He told me that he walked around the body to go to the front door to let additional firemen inside. Since her head was next to the counter, he walked around her feet. Therefore, he was the one who left the scuff marks in the soot around her feet. A couple of days later I called him back as I had another question for him. His response was, "I don't remember anything". Someone had shut him up.

That, too, was shrugged off by the County Attorney.

He then reached into his desk drawer and pulled out a few pictures of the crime scene that included images of Pearl's burnt body and the surrounding room. He cautioned us that these pictures were graphic and hard to look at.

They were. But I felt strong enough to handle it.

But we were disappointed that he had only a few pictures out of the 45 that supposedly existed. This troubled me greatly and I couldn't shake the feeling that these were purposefully being withheld from me. On June 6, 2016, I wrote the County Attorney a letter thanking him for taking time out of his busy day to meet with us. I also requested a second meeting to review the rest of the pictures. That same day, I wrote a letter to the County Medical Examiner in the Twin Cities (where the second inquest was held). Here is what I wrote.

Good afternoon,
Last week I met with our local County Attorney regarding the suspicious death of Pearl Justice in 1993. Recently, I've had the opportunity to review some of the crime scene photos and pictures taken during the investigation. I also gained access to the Coroner's Inquest documentation from your office. As a witness in this case, I was not asked to be present at your questioning during the Inquest. I have several unanswered questions that I believe you could help me get clarity on. Would it be possible to schedule a meeting with you at your earliest convenience? I can be reached by phone or mail.
Looking forward to hearing back from you.
Jeanie Hall

The Medical Examiner did eventually call me, and we had a long conversation about his findings. I contradicted some of his statements from the inquest. Regarding the crime scene photos, I asked him why there were scuff marks in the soot around her body. He recalled that when he looked at the photos, he deduced that she was alive after the fire. He had not been told that the first fireman to enter Pearl's house that morning had walked around her body to open the front door for the rest of his team and left scuff marks in the soot. That same fireman had also picked up the smoldering pillow on the chair by her body (the one I suspected had been used to suffocate her and end her life) and threw it out the back door into the snow.

The medical examiner then told me that he would need an order from the County Attorney or the police department to be able to reopen, and reexamine, this case.

The day after our conversation, the County Attorney left me a voicemail and informed me that he would not meet with me again. He would, however, scan and send me the remaining crime scene photos. Within days, I had the photos in my possession. On June 11, 2016, I sent another letter to the County Attorney and the Medical Examiner thanking them for their time and assistance. But this letter was more than a "thank you." It was a four-page document that listed the many unanswered questions and anomalies in Pearl's case that were yet to be explained.

I received no reply from either official... and likely never will.

Here are few of the dozens of questions that I feel need to be explained or investigated:

- The first officer on the scene noted Pearl's front door was unlocked. Pearl never left her door unlocked at night. Why was it unlocked?
- The first officer on the scene noted the damage to the frame around the front door. The investigating deputy claimed that the door was damaged when the first fireman made entry. Why would the fireman damage a door that was already open?
- Pearl's personal documents were found in a black garbage bag at the scene and there were indications that accelerants had been poured on them. Why would Pearl put important documents like her late husband's death certificate in a garage bag, and then pour flammable liquid on it?

- The liquid on the papers was tested and tested positive for petroleum distillate (a highly flammable accelerant), yet why did this not raise any red flags with the police?
- I reported that I had seen a flicker of light through Pearl's window at midnight. Why was this information omitted from the investigating officer's report? Spent matchsticks were found strewn around the house and 10 boxes of matchsticks were found in the house.
- There were cloth fibers embedded in Pearl's throat that were similar to the cushion (the one the fireman threw outside) that could have been used to smother her and end her life. Why was this connection never made? Why wasn't the cushion examined or preserved as evidence?
- The Fire Marshal and the investigating officer disagree on the path of the fire. Why was this not clarified?
- Deputies never conducted a door-to-door investigation at the surrounding neighbors. Why did that not take place?
- The fire was attributed to the can of cooking grease on the stove, yet evidence of petroleum distillate was on the floor near and around her body. Why did this not raise red flags to the authorities?
- The investigating officer and the Fire Marshal stated that Pearl's death was the result of a heart attack, yet no mention of "heart attack" is present in the reports.
- The crime scene reports note that there was "blood spatter on the counter with blood transfer noted." Why is there blood? Was a blow to the head involved in her death?

This list could go on and on.

But after my requests for further information and investigation went unanswered, the dreaded realization hit me that it was likely that Pearl's murderers would never be brought to justice. No matter how hard I tried, no one believed me, and the police and the court systems just wanted me to go away.

My summary of that night is simple: Two men were sent by my ex-husband to retrieve the damning evidence against him and the attorneys that was in my possession. These men broke into the wrong house, piled any papers that looked important into a garbage bag, and doused it with accelerant. Their intentions were to destroy evidence while also burning my house down and scaring me into silence forever.

But they made a deadly mistake. They went to the wrong house and were caught in the act by Pearl. They panicked, argued with her, and ultimately decided to cover their tracks by eliminating her as a witness. A struggle ensued and, being elderly and frail, Pearl was beaten, knocked down to the ground, and smothered into unconsciousness with the cushion. The fire served as the means to cover up their mistake.

I know this with every fiber of my being because I was there. It was supposed to be me, and I saw this heinous mistake in living color that night from my property. As the years ticked by and I immersed myself in my own investigation of her death, all the pieces of the puzzle fit together. I could see, clear as day, that it was murder.

I only wish the people in positions of power could see that as well.

My last recourse and act of kindness in honor of Pearl is to write my story in detail and in 100% truth. Once this book is published, I know readers will see what I see and validate what I have known for thirty years. I have no more ill feelings toward those who investigated her death in every facet, but I do hope they learn from the errors made during the mistaken closed case of Pearl Justice.

If I could have one wish, it would be that no other person on this planet needs to endure the mayhem, hurt, and fear that I have experienced over my lifetime.

Chapter 19

The Healer and the Healing

AFTER THE TRAGIC DEATH OF MY FRIEND Pearl and the unexpected death of my only son, I was no longer bold, brave, or determined. I was shattered and numb. During the writing of this story, I often worried that I was putting "too much God" into the retelling of the last 28 years of my life. But I also cannot deny that His strength and presence have brought me through unimaginable pain.

God was my strength even during the darkest of times, but I neglected to seek his help. I forgot this important Bible verse through all my times of struggle and chaos:

Be strong and courageous for wherever you go, I am there.
—JOSHUA 1:8-9

I constantly felt as if I were still forging into battle alone. I was still working as a nurse at the nearby hospital. I worked as many shifts as I could, but they were mainly evenings and weekends so I could avoid other staff members and doctors as much as possible. Being around my patients was a pleasant reprieve and kept my mind busy and my heart full.

I was always on the fence between "calm me" and "sobbing me" most days. I could barely socialize with others and withdrew more and more every day. Even joyful events like weddings, picnics, and family gatherings sent me into emotional overload. I liken it to being on the top ledge of a skyscraper in a windstorm with every ounce of my energy dedicated to not falling off the edge.

Attending Sunday service at church was another thing that was too much for my shattered emotions to bear. My faith was shaken, and I couldn't bring myself to navigate a crowd of people who were joyously singing and praying while my soul felt crushed. A friend told me I needed to figure out why I was withdrawing from gatherings. I eventually stopped going to church because it brought all my sad feelings bubbling to the surface, and I would end up sitting in the pew quietly crying. I was not angry at God, but I wondered *why? Why did this happen to me?*

The guilt and confusion were overwhelming.

I found it easier to be by myself instead of embarrassing myself with floods of tears. I felt I had already made a fool of myself plenty of times trying to tell the police and the County Attorney what I had witnessed. Every time I tried the words would not come out, but the tears would. As a result, I was unable to communicate effectively what had happened and so no one believed me. The circumstances surrounding the murder seemed too complicated for most people to understand. But the path that led to a case of mistaken identity . . . which then led to Pearl's murder . . . was crystal clear to me. It was a frustrating cycle of grief and guilt.

I occasionally wondered if people were whispering behind my back, "Pearl was just a neighbor, so why is she having such a hard time getting over her death?"

If this was the case back then, or even now, I can promise the naysayers that there is a whole other level of hell with a side order of paralyzing fear when you truly believe that someone else took the death blows that were meant for you.

Back then the fear never left me that the murderers would still try to come back a second time to finish the job. This type of paralyzing fear clings to you like glue and weighs heavily on your mind, body, and spirit.

Chapter 20

I'm Doing Better Now

Have you ever stopped and wondered what God has done in your life that you aren't aware of?

Maybe He healed you before you were even sick. Perhaps He saved you from a fatal car crash that never happened. I feel like God has protected me more times than I can count, so I can only imagine the times He's rescued me when I wasn't aware that I was in danger. I thank Him for watching over me, even when I didn't realize it. What an awesome God we serve. Amen.

—JAMES DIXON

As of the writing of this book, I can share that I am "OK" as well. I am still carrying a lot of guilt about Pearl's death, but the grief is lessening. My life continues to be a rollercoaster of emotions, but I know now that I am a fighter and a survivor. I've changed and grown a lot in nearly three decades

I now realize that the police, fire department, and investigators, probably lacked the experience and training to do a thorough investigation. Even though I know one of the perpetrators from the night of December 22, 1993, is still alive, I no longer fear retaliation from him.

It is also my hope that these agencies learn from the mistakes they made with me personally and even while conducting their investigations. "Sensitivity Training" for officers and elected officials was not available in the 1990s, but I wish it had been. I can only hope that others who find themselves in circumstances like mine are not dismissed, ridiculed, and ignored as I was during the years of my divorce and during the investigation of Pearl's house fire.

My love for horses has never changed, with one exception. For years I clung to my horses because they were my life. At one time, I owned 22. The first year I bought my farm, I bred nine mares hoping to get six foals. Instead, I was blessed with nine little darlings. After they were weaned, I hung nine little colorful buckets on the paddock fences for their grain. It looked like a scene that should be in a national magazine or a travel calendar.

Then, in 2019, I woke up one morning with the strong sense that I didn't need 22 horses for strength anymore. I was strong enough to start letting them go to new homes and new owners who would love them. Slowly but surely, I whittled my numbers down from 22 to six.

The number of animals I personally own may be fewer, but the horses I do own are all trained by me. Over the years, my thoroughbreds have brought in seven-win pictures. My biggest joy is being a breeder. I love watching the babies come into this world and I love being part of their growth and training. When I sit in a grandstand at a racetrack and watch one of my "babies" trot out onto the track, it's always a proud mommy moment.

People often find it amusing that, during a time in life when others are enjoying retirement, I'm enjoying raising thoroughbred racehorses and watching them become successful on the track.

Another thing I let go of was my nursing career. I retired from my work as a nurse in 2011 and tried to settle into a slower-paced life. Despite not working in the medical field anymore or owning a huge herd, I keep plenty busy.

Around 2016, I became good friends with an amazing woman named Deanna who had a knack for writing. It was she who encouraged me to revisit this 27-year ordeal and put it into story form. She also had great insight into my behavior and actions during the years between the early 1980s and early 2000s. She understood the choices I made and actually heard me (and believed me) when I retold the story of December 22, 1993.

I had been working on the story of my life for years and had almost 100 pages of journaling and thoughts neatly typed. Along with that, I had hundreds of documents connected to the investigation (or lack thereof) of Pearl's death. With Deana's support, I began to see these pieces of paper as not only an incredible story for others to read, but a key piece of my final healing.

Another writer friend reviewed my notes for this story and sent back a lovely reply of encouragement. She also summed up my essence in a way that only an accomplished writer could.

"This woman, a natural woman, horse-rider, a woman filled with experiences, wisdom, and a love for all living things. Her other voice is naïve, too patient as many abused people seem to make themselves as they are caught up in webs of lies. And then there is her third voice: one that is compulsive and the accumulator of facts.

This woman is a survivor, no question. And valuable. In her story, I see a juxtaposition of the trusting noble animals, the beauty of nature and seasons, the hard life of farming, the struggle against ignoble con artists, and a lying and cheating man who didn't care what he did to others.

Her story is also one of a woman navigating an internal struggle for vindication and what's right."

This is my story: a story of the tragic loss of a friend, heartache, murder, trauma, conspiracy, lies, elusive justice, a case that should have never been marked "closed," and my rising from the ashes of all of it.

The names and places have been changed, for various reasons. The main reason for anonymity is that Pearl's death was ruled an accident despite glaring inconsistencies and endless questions.

I was witness to the events that led to the ending of her life by evil men that night. To this day, I know with every fiber of my being that the man responsible still lives free and unpunished.

My intent with this story is not to bring the guilty to justice, "stir the pot," or cause drama and heartache. My intent is to tell the story . . . the whole story . . . of the events and people that ultimately led to the killers going one driveway too far and ending the life of the wrong woman.

This is my story. I *know* what I have been through. I *see* the pieces of this crime that began years prior and ended in the most brutal and unjust way. I *see* what authorities, family members, and the law did not see.

I *saw* who took Pearl's life that night. I *heard* their arguments and confession to each other loud and clear in the crisp midnight air. I *saw* their faces clearly from the safety of my hiding spot on the backside of Pearl's property.

I can also promise you that none of the information you read in this story is fabricated or embellished in any way. This is not fiction. This is a true story. Over the last 28 years, I have documented, researched, and saved hundreds of legal, court, and law enforcement documents surrounding the following events of my life.

My life has been filled with many traumatic events, including the death of my beloved son at a young age. But the realization that has hit me hard late in life is that, when you are barely surviving, you do not dream. After this tragedy, I now believe that I have been suffering from PTSD.

It's time for me to dream and start living again. Once I type "The End" on this story of death, darkness, courage, and healing, I will not look back any longer.

Only ahead. THE END.

Epilogue

I KNOW THERE WILL BE NO FURTHER investigation into the murder of my neighbor, and it will remain a "closed case" in the eyes of the authorities. But I take great comfort in knowing that, as I close this chapter of my life, I can look to the heavens and say, "Pearl, I tried." Whether you, the reader, believe me or not is irrelevant. My intent with this true-crime, nonfiction, and part-memoir book is to make my version of this murder known and have my voice heard.

I've been asked what happened to the people that I've talked about in this book. My first husband remarried and has since passed away. My second husband (Ed) passed away about ten years ago. His wife preceded him in death and died at home. The fake appraiser lives in Wisconsin, and the former manager of the Full-Service Car Wash, Roger Hammer, has also passed. Even as the end of their days neared, they both refused to acknowledge the events of the night of December 22, 1993.

The whereabouts of my attorney, Ross Irwin, are unknown, but I honestly don't care. He must live with the sins and memory of how he treated me (and probably others as well). That is his burden to carry.

As of the publishing of this book, I have achieved the milestone of 80 trips around the sun. In my many decades on Earth, I learned many things.

- I learned that evil will triumph if it is unchallenged.
- I learned that men of power and money will steamroll right over the top of you if you
- let them.
- I learned that being labeled as "crazy" doesn't take much in the eyes of some law
- enforcement.
- I have learned that the scars you **don't see** are the ones that take the longest to
- fade.
- But I also learned that light will eventually overcome the dark.
- I learned that God is great, and family is everything.
- I also learned that I **do** have a voice, that I **do** have a backbone, and I **do** have the
- power to stand up for myself and demand change.
- I learned that my horses are actually four-legged angels with fur and hooves.
- I learned who my friends are, who my enemies are, and which ones to keep close.
- I learned to not let the opinions of people who don't matter much, matter much.
- I learned that I have friends in unique places.
- I learned that I have more supporters and cheerleaders than I had ever dreamed
- possible.
- I learned that heartache will mend, even if it takes surgery to help it along.

Depression is anger turned inward, so I have learned to forgive. I am still working on forgiving those who have treated me poorly and wronged me over the years, because hate is too heavy of a load to carry into my final chapter of life. I recognize the value of being controlled by my conscience because it means I cannot tell a lie even if I wanted to.

This concludes my retelling of the events that ultimately led to mistaken identity and tragedy around midnight of December 22, 1993. And the nearly three-decade journey to healing that has followed.

With the publishing of this book, I have done all that I can to bring justice to my friend. On that night of December 22, 1993, there were two victims; one lived, and one did not. It has taken me 28 gut-wrenching, mental health-shattering years to finally feel like I am rising up from this mess and beginning to heal.

I am doing better now. I now live close to my family and see my sister and daughter regularly. Life is good. Thank you for taking the time to read Pearl's and my story.

"My soul searches desperately for the longings of my heart, and the fear that my dreams may never be."

—SOURCE UNKNOWN

About the Author

IN 1991, I BEGAN TO TELL MY STORY BY putting it on a three-hour tape. I named this story, "So Help Me God." In 1993, my neighbor, Pearl was murdered when the intruders went to the wrong house. I have spent 28 years trying to inform the authorities that Pearl was murdered by mistake. My story is now complete, and it has taken me 30 years to write.

Certified Civil Trial Specialist

May 19, 1989

Re: ██████████ Defense of Lawsuits Commenced by █████

Gentlemen:

As you are aware, I have been representing Mr ██████ over the past several years in the defense of the many lawsuits which have arisen out of the failure of ███ ████████

At the present time, ████████████████████████████ is pursuing this matter after having received an assignment of ████████████████████ and the interest of the SBA. ████████████████ is being represented by ████████████████.

Mr. ██████ has a good defense to several of the notes running in favor of ████████████████████ on the grounds that they were forged by a bank officer who, as you will recall, then proceeded to burn down the bank to hide his illegal activities in this file as well as other bank customer files. Unfortunately, Mr. ██████ does not have a defense to his personal guarantee of SBA loan number ██████████████████ dated February 25, 1982 in the principal sum of $340,000 with interest at the rate of 18¼ percent per annum. Mr ██████ was careful to sign most of the other notes which are admittedly his as president of the corporation; however, there's no getting around the fact that he is on the hook for the major note, a copy of which I append hereinafter for your information.

At a pre-trial conference in this matter held in ██████████ before the Honorable ████████████ on April 4, 1989, ████████████ gave Mr. ██████ 20 days to amend his pleadings with 10 days on our part to respond. Thereafter, Mr. ██████ is to submit a Note of Issue/Certificate of Readiness in this matter and the matter will be deemed ready to be called for trial.

```
                        Activity Summary                    _____
                                                                           Firs

███████████             Dissolution w/o Chil        Date filed: 01/14/198

         vs. ████████████████████
_____
  Date    Activity              Start/End   Judge           Crt Rm Chrgs Cont
_ 01/14/88 Case Filed           01:25 01:25
                     CONVERTED 10/10/90 LAST DOC. 32
_ 10/11/90 Clerical             08:55
                     102690 DFT 0230 00260G 3
_ 10/26/90 Clerical             02:10
                     ████████████ CALLED TO CONTINUE 102690 DFT
                     HE WILL CALL TO RESCHEDULE
_ 11/02/90 Schdl Hrg            09:54
                     SCHEDULE FOR DEFAULT HEARING ASAP AT REQUEST OF ████████
_ 11/05/90 Clerical             11:16                                      D
                     ██████████ UNAVAILABLE FOR DFT HEARING HE SCHEDULED.
_ 11/20/90 Schdl Hrg            04:31
_ 11/21/90 Clerical             11:32
                     OK W/ ████████████ TO HEAR 122190 DFT
                     113090 - REQUEST BY ██████████
_ 11/30/90 Deflt Hrg            08:15      G Ring            3
_ 01/07/91 Doc. Filed           08:39
                     33. STIPULATION (LAH)
_ 01/07/91 Doc. Filed           09:15
                     34. FINDINGS OF FACT, CONCLUSIONS OF LAW, ORDER FOR JUDGMEN'
                         AND JUDGMENT AND DECREE - CLERK'S NOTICE (LAH)
_ 01/07/91 Closed               09:16
_ 07/07/91 Archive
=============================Pending Activities ==============================
  05/16/97 Archive             08:46 08:46
```

County Attorney's Office
Courthouse
████████████

TELEPHONE ████████████
FAX

April 25, 1996

████████████

Dear ████████

Enclosed herewith please find the law enforcement investigative material created in connection with the death of Pearl ████████. These are being provided to you pursuant to your request of April 15, 1996 for investigative materials in a now closed law enforcement investigation. I however am unable to provide you any copies of the reports of the Ramsey County Medical Examiner as those remain to be confidential information. A copy of said records can be obtained by the family members of Pearl ████████ by contacting the Ramsey County Medical Examiner's office, whose address is: 300 East University Avenue, St. Paul, MN 55101.

I can provide some general information concerning the autopsy however which would will useful should the family members wish to acquire a copy of the same. Said information is as follows:

Descendant's name:	Pearl ████████
Age:	86 year
Sex:	Female
Race:	Caucasian
Death:	12/22/93
Time:	0852 hours
Date of Examine:	12/23/93
Time:	1100 hours
Place of Death:	████████████
Pathologist:	
Place of Examine:	Ramsey County Medical Examiner's office
Medical Examiners	██████

Should you have any questions or concerns about the above please feel free to contact me at any time.

Very truly yours,

████████████

████████
County Attorney

████████

CASS COUNTY SHERIFF'S DEPARTMENT
WALKER, MINNESOTA

(INITIAL COMPLAINT REPORT)

I.C.R. NUMBER _____

OFFENSE: _____ House fire _____ STATUTE: _____

TIME REC'D: _____ 0852 __ REC'D BY _____ 304 ____ DATE REC'D _____ 122293 __ 19 ____

REPORTED BY: _____ ████████ _____ HOME PHONE: ████████

ADDRESS: _____ ████████ _____ WORK PHONE: _____

COMPLAINANT: _____ HOME PHONE: _____

ADDRESS: _____ WORK PHONE: _____

TOWNSHIP OR VILLAGE: __ Other jurisdiction _____ GRID ____ ████

DATE OCCURED: _____ 122293 __ TIME OCCURED: ___ 0852 _____ HOW REC'D: ___ Phone 911

PERSON ATTACKED: _____ HOW ATTACKED: _____

PROPERTY ATTACKED: _____ HOW ATTACKED: _____

WEAPON TYPE and HOW USED: _____

PROPERTY AND VALUE (stolen or arson) _____

PERSON ARRESTED / TAGGED: _____ DOB: _____

SEX: _____ RACE: _____ HGT: _____ WGT: _____ HAIR: _____ EYES: _____

ADDRESS: _____ D.L. # : _____

EMPLOYER: _____

COMPLAINT: _____ States he stopped at the Pearl ████████ residence and opened the doo
and the house was full of smoke. ████████████████████████
████████████████

DISPOSITION: _____ Referred to Crow wing county.

FAxed To Fire MARSHALL 815 ow 12-22-93 AT 2210 HRS. - 303,

OFFICER ASSG'N: _____ 680/209/111 TIME ASSG'N: __ 0852 ____ TIME ARR: 0903 ____ TIME CLR: 1034

ISN: __ 01 ____ MOC: 9201 ___ USC: S _____ ISN: _____ MOC: _____ USC: _____

ISN: _____ MOC: _____ USC: _____ ISN: _____ MOC: _____ USC: _____

ISN: _____ MOC: _____ USC: _____ ISN: _____ MOC: _____ USC: _____

ADDITIONAL REPORTS: _____ ENTERED CJIS: _____ ENTERED 3Y: _____

VOLUNTARY STATEMENT
(NOT UNDER ARREST)

I,█████████████████████████████████, am not under arrest for, nor am I being detained for any crim

offenses concerning the events I am about to make known to __DEPUTY█████████████__
Without being accused of or questioned about any criminal offenses regarding the facts I am about to state, I volunteer the
lowing information of my own free will, for whatever purposes it may serve.

I am_____years of age, and I live at _____

Q: Ahh, the time on this is ahh, 1008 hours. The date is 12-22-96. This is Deputy █████

█████ I am in my squad car at a fire scene located approximately one mile south of

███████████████████ Sitting here with me is the gentleman who found or

discovered this fire. Sir, can I have your full name, middle name, date of birth?

A: It's █████████████, ahh....

Q: How do you spell that?

A: It's ████████, and my birth date is 12-13-61. Ahh,...

Q: Address?

A: It's ahh, ████████████████████████████, Minnesota ████.

Q: Your telephone number?

A: It's ahh, area code ███████.

Q: What can you tell me? What happened here?

A: Well, I was stoppin' to make my normal ahh, deliveries....

Q: What time would that have been?

A: Must have been about 8:30 approximately (inaudible) think with 10 minutes going, about 8:3

or so and ahh, I came up to the house and I could see some smoke rolling out of the window

Q: Front window or back window? Or which one?

A: The...kind of a kitchen window.

Q: That in the front or on the side? I haven't been up to the scene yet.

A: On the side of the house.

have read each page of this statement consisting of __4__ page(s), each page of which bears my signature, and corrections,
ıny, bear my initials, and I certify that the facts contained herein are true and correct.

)ated at _____, this_____day of_____19____

VITNESS:_____

/ITNESS:_____   _____
                                           Signature of person giving voluntary statement.

STATEMENT OF: ▓▓▓▓▓▓▓▓ Date 12-22-93 Page No. 3

DOB: ▓▓▓▓▓

Q: How old is she?

A: I would say about 80....roughly.

Q: She live there by herself?

A: Ahh, as far as I know.

Q: How long have you been servicing the residence here?

A: Umm, probably about a year.

Q: Okay. (radio transmission). So then ahh, you stayed here until the fire department cam

A: Right.

Q: Do you have any idea what, you know, a,a, when you were in there looking at the fire or the short time you were in there, do you ahh, did you surmise what of may have happened?

A: Umm, it's possible she had a, ahh, something on the stove that caught on fire and you know.

Q: Okay. I was just wondering if there was something that you recall now as we're talking.

A: Oh.

Q: ....seeing....you were in there twice now, right?

A: Yeah. Well....

Q: Okay. That....

A: Kind of. Yeah.

Q: Yeah. That...is...that you recall now as we're talking the, that ya, that tripped your trigger as to oh, I'll bet that's what started the fire or whatever. There wasn't anything that you can recall?

A: No. Noth, nothing stands out I guess.

Q: Okay. Were you scheduled to make a stop here today?

A: Yes, I was.

Q: Do you normally stop at this time?

A: Yes.

Q: Is there anything we haven't covered that you can think to add to this?

▓▓▓▓▓ 22293

STATEMENT OF: ████████████ DOB: ████████

A: (inaudible) Umm, ...umm, I guess not.

Q: Alright. The time is ahh, 1013 and this statement is complete.

████/122293

VOLUNTARY STATEMENT
(NOT UNDER ARREST)

I,_____, am not under arrest for, nor am I being detained for any crim

offenses concerning the events I am about to make known to_____DEPUTY ████████_____

Without being accused of or questioned about any criminal offenses regarding the facts I am about to state, I volunteer the
lowing information of my own free will, for whatever purposes it may serve.

I am_____years of age, and I live at_____

Q: The time is ahh, 1018, date is 12-22 and this would be a (ringing noise in background) ta

   regarding the fire scene located on ███████████ approximately 1 mile south of the junc

   of County Road███████ This is Deputy ██████████. I'm g'be talking to one of the fi

   and, at the scene here. Sir, can I get your name please?

A: Ahh, ████████████

Q: ████, what's your middle name?

A: ████. ████████████. (clears throat).

Q: Okay, and your date of birth?

A: Ahh, ████████

Q: And what's your address?

A: Ahh, ████████████.

Q: Okay. Telephone number?

A: ████████

Q: I talked to the gentleman that ahh, found the fire....

A: (clears throat).

Q: ..████. His name was a ████ ...I'll get it here... ██████████. He said that he ahh, h

   knocked on the door, he initially pulled in, he saw smoke rolling from ahh, what appeared

   to be a window, ahh, beat on the door for a couple seconds, opened the door, ahh, didn't

   see any, well the only flame he states that he saw was like sparks on the, on the ahh,

   carpeting in the kitchen or in the living room. I wasn't quite clear on that. When I

I have read each page of this statement consisting of __3__ page(s), each page of which bears my signature, and correction:
any, bear my initials, and I certify that the facts contained herein are true and correct.

Dated at_____. this_____day of_____19____

WITNESS:_____

WITNESS:_____

████████   Signature of person giving voluntary statement.

████/122293

Date 12-22-93   Page No. 2

STATEMENT OF: ██████████   DOB: ██████

Q: questioned further on it, he said it was like it was smouldering but he did state that saw a lady by the name Pearle, he knows as the person that resides here, on the floor, looked like she was dead. At that point, he went and called the fire department. What have you guys discovered?

A: Well, when we pulled in, the, this guy was sitting out on the road waiting for us when we got here. Ahh, we pulled in. I went to the front door, felt that. There was no he ahh, living room window was cold. Went around to the back door and felt that. There w no heat. Ahh, opened the door and I could see her laying on the floor and it was quite apparent that way she was dead so we didn't, we didn't touch nothing, just you know, just left it the way it was. There was...absolutely no fire at all. It had burt itsel out and ahh, we, we really did nothing except open the door and looked in and found her (clears throat).

Q: What, what do you think happened? Any idea?

A: Ummm, there was a burner on on the stove underneath ahhh, what appeared to be like a two pound coffee can. Ahh, we s, we did shut that off. Umm, apparently she was cooking something on the stove and....from there I don't know, ahh, that, but she was definatel using the stove.

Q: Ah huh (positive response).

A: Umm, there was a pillow smouldering on one of the chairs in the kitchen. just a cushion pillow. Ahh, I took, you know, took that out. Umm, that's about it. Ahh, the s, step well I shouldn't say step-daughter...daughter-in-law and a granddaughter were here on scene when we arrived also.

Q: They were? Okay.

A: Yeah. Umm, (clears throat) but they were not here initially when the guy discovered him

Q: Um huh (positive response).

A: They live just around the corner and they heard it on their scanner and jumped in thei car and came over here.

STATEMENT OF: ▆▆▆▆▆▆▆▆ DOB: ▆▆▆▆ Date 12-22-93 Page No. 3

Q: Okay, so relatives have been notified then or they're aware...

A: Yeah, the...his son and, and daughter-in-law and granddaughter were here. Her son I should say.

Q: Okay. Okay how, ahh, so at this point, you don't know, of course you haven't checked anything, you've left everything but ahh, you don't really know ahhh, what the cause o the fire was other than that there was a burner but umm, something had to have caught right?

A: Right. Yeah. There ahh, the cabinets up above the stove and stuff are burnt and ahh, the patch around her on the living room carpet or the kitchen carpet, pardon me, umm and the house had been real hot. There's candles melted way into the living room.

Q: Oh.

A: And there was a lot of heat at one time but it, it had burnt itself out.

Q: Okay. Is there anything we haven't covered?

A: Ahh, not that I'm aware of. There is a (clears throat) one of the kitchen windows is cracked open maybe half an inch and you know, whether she...maybe she, you know, ahh, h tried to open that to get rid of the smoke if, you know, I, you know that's speculatior of course. Umm, but that's a possibility.

Q: How was she dressed? She dressed in a nightgown or...

A: Umm, there's no clothing left on her what-so-ever now. She's.....

Q: It...burned off?

A: It's all burnt off, yes. There's ahh, ahh, there's...I couldn't, you know, we didn't touch her of course but there's no visible shreds of nothing...right now.

Q: Okay.

A: (clears throat).

Q: Okay. Very good. The time is 1022 and this statement is complete.

███████ COUNTY LAW ENFORCEMENT CENTER
SUPPLEMENTARY REPORT

MN0180000   CASE NR ███████

Complainant: ███████████ - Deputy Sheriff
             ███████ County Sheriff's Department

Offense: Death Investigation

Page Nr: 1 of 4   Date: 12/23/93

SYNOPSIS

The following report contains information about a residence fire
which occurred in ████████ Township. An adult female was found
dead at the scene of the fire. The fire scene was investigated by
the ██████████ County Sheriff's Department and the State Fire
Marshall's Office. See details section.

Agency: ████████ County Sheriff's Department
                 Minnesota State Fire Marshall's Office
                 ████████ County Coroner's Office
                 ████ Ambulance Service
                 ████████ Fire Department
                 Ramsey County Coroner's Office

Officers: ██████████, Sheriff's Investigator
                 ██████████, Sheriff's Investigator
                 ██████████ Deputy Fire Marshall
                 ██████████, Deputy Sheriff

Deceased: Pearl ██████████   dob 12/4/08
                 ██████████.
                 residence located on CR ██ - Fire number ████

Others: ████████████
                 ████████████████
                 ████████████

Details: 12/22/93 at 0923hrs. The ██████████ County Sheriff's
Department received a report from the ████████ Sheriff's
Department about a house fire in ████████████. The report
indicated that there was a deceased person in the residence.

12/22/93 at 1011hrs. Deputy ████████ arrived at the fire scene.
The residence was located on ████████ and had a fire number of
████ Upon arrival Deputy ████████ noted that the ██████████
Department was on the scene. Also present at the scene was
Assistant ████████ County Coroner ████████, Sheriff's
Deputies ████████ and ██████████, and ████ Ambulance
Service personnel. Deputy Fire Marshall ██████████ arrived a
short time later.

Deputy ████████ noted that there was no active fire in the residence
at this time. The fire scene appeared to be cold and was confined

INVESTIGATING OFFICER(S): ████████
REPORT MADE BY: ████████   DATE:12/23/93
CASE FILED: Y/N THIS CASE IS:CLEARED BY ARREST/UNFOUNDED/INACTIVE/OTHE

```
            ▓▓▓▓▓▓▓ COUNTY LAW ENFORCEMENT CENTER
                   SUPPLEMENTARY REPORT
 MN0180000
                                   CASE NR▓▓▓▓▓
```

| Complainant: ▓▓▓▓▓▓ - Deputy Sheriff |
| ▓▓▓▓▓ County Sheriff's Department |

Offense: Death Investigation

Page Nr: 2 of 4   Date: 12/23/93

to the kitchen area of the residence. Deputy ▓▓▓▓ then photographed the scene with a video camera. Still photographs were also taken by Deputy ▓▓▓▓.

While at the scene Deputy ▓▓▓▓ learned that the ▓▓▓▓▓ Fire Department received the call of the fire at 0852hrs. They responded to the scene and found the fire to be cold. They did not have to extinguish any portion of the fire. Deputy ▓▓▓ learned that Deputy ▓▓▓▓ obtained a taped statement from fireman ▓▓▓▓▓. Deputy ▓▓▓▓ also obtained a taped statement from ▓▓▓▓▓. He is a Schwann's delivery person and discovered the fire.

Deputy ▓▓▓ learned from firemen at the scene that the stove and oven were both on at the time of their arrival. One fireman noted that he turned the knob on the stove to the off position. This was the knob that controlled the power to the right rear burner. Deputy ▓▓▓ noted that there was a large coffee type can on the right rear burner that contained a grease type substance. There was also a frying pan on the right front burner and a muffin tin with muffins in it on the top left side of the stove. The oven was on and set at 350 degrees and there was a muffin tin with muffins in it.

Deputy ▓▓▓ observed a body on the floor of the kitchen in a prone position. The body appeared to have substantial burn-type injuries. The decedents eyeglasses were in the general area of the head but were damaged and in pieces. Deputy ▓▓▓ was unable to determine if there was any clothing on the body at this time. The body was transported to ▓▓▓▓ Medical Center by ▓▓▓ Ambulance Service.

Deputy ▓▓▓ observed a spent stick-type match on the kitchen counter near the refrigerator. Two other non-spent matches were located in the kitchen area. One was on the floor and one was in the sink. There was a candle on the counter in the kitchen. The kitchen area was searched for any other object that required some type of fire but none was found.

Deputy Fire Marshall ▓▓▓▓▓ detected a possible accelerant type fluid on some documents located in the garbage in the kitchen area. This garbage was located on the floor on the same side of the kitchen as the stove. The garbage can was not present and was later located outside on the deck. The garbage appeared to be in a plastic bag. The documents located in the garbage were personal documents including tax-type information and her husbands death certificate. These documents were collected by ▓▓▓▓ for

```
 INVESTIGATING OFFICER(S): ▓▓▓▓
 REPORT MADE BY: ▓▓▓▓                    DATE:12/23/93
 CASE FILED: Y/N  THIS CASE IS:CLEARED BY ARREST/UNFOUNDED/INACTIVE/OTHE
```

LAW ~~ENFORCEMENT~~ CENTER
SUPPLEMENTARY REPORT

MN0180000 .   .   CASE NR: ██████

| Complainant: ██████████ - Deputy Sheriff |
| ██████████ County Sheriff's Department |

Offense: Death Investigation

Page Nr: 3 of 4   Date: 12/23/93

analysis. ██████████ also detected possible accelerant in the
carpet area of the kitchen. He also collected samples of the
carpet for analysis. Deputy ██████ located a plastic container of
paint thinner in the basement of the residence. Deputy ██████
noted that the paint thinner had a similar odor to the substance
on the documents in the garbage.

Deputy ██████ checked the residence inside and outside. There did
not appear to be anything out of order. It did not appear as if
anybody had gone through the residence to search for valuables.
There was no sign of tampering on the exterior. The doors and
windows were in tact with no sign of damage. The front door was
damaged but it was determined that the fire department forced
entry through this door. Deputy ██████████ checked the neighboring
residences to determine if they had any contact with Pearl
██████

The deceased was identified as Pearl ██████████ dob 12/4/08.
She was the sole occupant of the residence. This information was
obtained from Assistant Coroner ██████████

12/22/93 at 1145hrs. Deputy ██████ talked to ██████████ He
was identified as the son of Pearl ██████████ He stated that his
mother had been in good spirits recently and had plans to attend a
church function on Friday. He said that his daughter had
attempted to call Pearl on the morning of 12/22/93 between
0830hrs. and 0900hrs. She tried several times but continued to
get a busy signal. He related that his mother had no life
insurance that he was aware of and that he had the records at his
residence. He believed that the house was deeded to him and his
sister. He said that his mother was with his family on the night
of 12/21/93 and was dropped off at her residence that night. His
wife later called and talked with Pearl. He did relate that Pearl
had congestive heart failure.

12/22/93 at 1745hrs. Deputy ██████ talked with ██████████ by
phone. He said that his son, ██████████, had picked-up Pearl on
the night of 12/21/93 and drove her to a family function. She was
wearing a black sweatshirt, a red turtleneck, and a pair of black
polyester type pants. Deputy ██████ also talked with ██████
██████ daughter, ██████████, by phone. She said that Pearl
generally wore a cotton or flannel night gown and she had a maroon
polyester robe. ██████████ related that she took Pearl home
at about 2030hrs. to 2045hrs. Pearl told her that she was going
to make some orange rolls. She had previously prepared the batter
and it was in the refrigerator. She related that she may be up
late baking them. When ██████ took her home she went inside of
the house and turned the lights on for her. She did not notice

INVESTIGATING OFFICER(S): ██████
REPORT MADE BY: ██████
CASE FILED: Y/N THIS CASE IS CLEARED BY ARREST/UNF██ DATE:12/23/93

MN0180000 SUPPLEMENTARY REPORT

CASE NR [redacted]

Complainant: [redacted] - Deputy Sheriff
[redacted] County Sheriff's Department

Offense: Death Investigation

Page Nr: 4 of 4

Date: 12/23/93

anything unusual when she was inside. When [redacted] left the residence she slipped on the deck. She said that Pearl called at about 2130hrs. and asked how she was.

On 12/23/93 Deputy [redacted] was present during the autopsy of Pearl [redacted]. The autopsy was conducted by Dr. [redacted] of the Ramsey County Medical Examiner's Office. (see report prepared by Dr. [redacted]

Conclusion: End to date.

INVESTIGATING OFFICER(S): [redacted] DAD 1-3-94
REPORT MADE BY: [redacted]
DATE:12/23/93
CASE FILED: Y/N THIS CASE IS:CLEARED BY ARREST/UNFOUNDED/INACTIVE/OTH

Case No. ▮▮▮▮▮▮▮

POLICE OFFICERS EVIDENTIARY NOTICE
(File with prosecutor)

Name of defendant: Death Investigation

Arresting Officer ▮▮▮▮▮▮

Date & Time of arrest: 12-22-93

Offenses: Items from house fire

deceased: Pearl ▮▮▮▮▮▮

List separately:

1. Physical evidence taken from defendant or in the area he had control over, or in any way belonging to him.
2. Statements, admissions, or words spoken by the defendant (be sure to include which statements were after Miranda and which statements were volunteered or in response to general inquiries)
3. Evidence (e.g. contraband, fruits or instrumentalities of a crime) discovered elsewhere because of defendant's statements.
4. Photo displays; line-ups; or other identification procedure used.

SUMMARIZE EACH ITEM OF EVIDENCE	Place taken or statement made	Officer present to testify	Subsequent chain of possession
1. (1) spent match	CRIS F#2209	▮▮▮▮▮	
2. (10) boxes matches (1) plastic container	CRIS F#2209	▮▮▮▮▮	
3. part full Paint Thinner (1) plastic container	CRIS F#2209	▮▮▮▮▮	
4. part full Cre Solv	CRIS F#2209	▮▮▮▮▮	
5.			
6.			
7.			
8.			
9.			
10.			
11.			
12.			

List separately for discovery purposes:
1. Statements of accomplices
2. Summary of oral statements made by any witness
3. All potential witnesses; their addresses; criminal record; any possible harm or coercion to them if name is disclosed.
4. Laboratory reports (actual or anticipated).

1. _____
2. _____
3. _____
4. _____
5. _____
6. _____

Case Number: ▮▮▮▮▮▮
Date of Incident: 12-22-93
Diagram By: ▮▮▮▮▮▮
Not to Scale

A = kitchen
B = deceased
C = stove
D = sink
E = garbage
F = living roo▮
G = bedroom
H = bathroom
I = bedroom
J = front door
K = side door

INVESTIGATION REPORT:

PEOPLE

Owner\Victim - Pearl ██████████, DOB 12-04-08; Route 1, ████████████████

Reporting Party - ████████████: ████████████████████████

████████████

Officer In Charge - ███████████: ████

Assisting Officers - Deputy ████████, Deputy ████████, Deputy ████████

████████ County Sheriff's Department, ████████████████

Deputy County Coroner - ███████████████████████

PRELIMINARY INFORMATION

At 0930 hours on December 22, 1993, I was contacted by the ████████ County Sheriff's Department and was asked to respond to ████████ for a fire investigation. I was also informed that there was the possibility of a death involved.

I arrived at the Pearl ████████ residence, ████████████, at 1000 hours and was met by Incident Commander ████████████, Deputy Coroner ████████, and Sheriff's Deputies ████████████. We discussed the circumstances surrounding the fire. I was informed that there was one victim, the homeowner, Pearl ████████ DOB 12-04-08.

BACKGROUND

At 0852 hours on December 22, 1993, the ████████ Sheriff's Department received a call from ████████ who stated that there was smoke coming from the Pearl ████████ residence on County Road ████.

The ████████ Fire Department was dispatched and, upon arrival, observed that there was no visible smoke showing. After entry to the house was made, the victim was found in the kitchen. Determining that the fire was out, the fire department removed itself from the scene and secured it until sheriff's deputies arrived. The Fire Marshal was then called.

PROPERTY DESCRIPTION

The fire occurred in a one story rambler measuring about 24' x 26'. The 2" x 4" wall studs were supported by the basement block walls and were covered with sheetrock and paneling on the interior and wood lap siding on the exterior. All the floors were carpeted,

1

except the bathroom, which was tiled. The house was fully furnished and was occupied prior to the fire. The house's electricity and heat were in operation prior to the fire.

EXTERIOR EXAMINATION

After conferring with the other authorities, I started my examination with a walk around the exterior. I observed that the house sustained no visible exterior fire damage. Exterior smoke damage was limited to a small area around the south kitchen window which was cracked open slightly. It appeared that the window had been open prior to the fire.

INTERIOR EXAMINATION

On the interior, I started my exam in the area of least fire damage and worked to the area with the most fire damage. Upon entering the structure, I noticed that the interior of the house was void of any lingering smoke or heat from the fire. This was unusual because smoke almost always lingers for a long time after the fire is extinguished. After an initial examination, it was evident that the house, at one time, did contain a large amount of smoke and heat. Although the entire house was smoked up at one time, the fire damage was confined to the kitchen area.

In the bedroom, I saw that the bed was not made. The bed spread was lying as to indicate that the bed was occupied before the fire. There was also an open book on the night stand next to the bed.

In the kitchen, I observed the victim on the floor. The victim appeared to be an elderly woman at least 80 years of age. She was lying with her stomach and face toward the floor. Her head rested against the kitchen base cabinets on the east side of the room, with her body at an angle toward the stove, which was located along the west wall. The victim's clothing had burned off during the fire. The victim appeared to suffer second and third degree burns to most of her body. The palm areas of both her hands were blistered and red. Her mouth and nose were also soot covered. The body was very stiff and cold. Lividity was present on her outer extremities.

Upon closer examination of the victim and surrounding area, I observed smeared finger marks on the edge of the kitchen counter, possibly indicating an attempt to get up or an attempt to break her fall. I also observed a long scratch in the base cabinet above her head. This fresh scratch was made by her eye glasses during her fall. The eye pieces to her glasses

2

were also in close proximity to her body. I took photographs of the body prior to it being moved.

In the kitchen, I observed most of the heavy fire damage to the cabinets to the left of the stove. This fire damage extended from the base cabinet up to the wall cabinet above. The carpet was also scorched around where the victim was found. This burn radiated back toward the stove. It appeared that the fire traveled from the victim, and where she lay on the carpet, toward the base cabinet by the stove. The ceiling area above the stove, while still intact, also sustained some heat and fire damage.

I examined the electric stove closer and found that two of the control knobs were still on. One of the knobs was for the oven and the other was for the right rear burner. On top of the stove, I saw a partially burned hot pad holder lying near a coffee can partially filled with some type of grease. This can was sitting on top of the right rear burner. The bottom of the can was darkened and scorched black. Also on the stove was a loaf of homemade bread and a pan of some type of muffins. Both were charred due to the fire.

There was a skillet on the right front burner. In the oven I observed another pan of muffins. These muffins were charred and black due to being over cooked. I took photographs of the kitchen area and stove.

I next examined the area where the trash had sat prior to the fire. This area was along side the cabinet which was next to the stove. The trash sat in a paper bag which was inside a plastic bag. The trash had been partially burned by the fire. While sifting through the trash, I noticed that the paper items were soaked with a liquid which smelled like paint thinner or mineral spirits. I examined the items closer and found them to be personal documents, including her husband's death certificate, check registers, and house papers. I took the mentioned items for chemical analysis.

EVIDENCE

On December 23, 1993, the following items were submitted to the B.C.A. for chemical analysis:

    Item 01 - debris from waste basket
    Item 02 - debris from waste basket
    Item 03 - carpet by stove
    Item 04 - carpet by stove

3

Item 05 - carpet by back door (control sample)

Item 06 - paint thinner from can found in basement (control sample)

Item 07 - carpet by victim

Also taken as evidence but *not* submitted for analysis:

Item 08 - paint thinner container from basement

Item 09 - dryer sheet found on basement door knob

Item 10 - cloth found on kitchen counter

Item 11 - cloth material found by victim on floor

Item 12 - cloth found in kitchen sink

On December 24, 1993, I spoke with ████████ from the B.C.A., who informed me that the samples had been tested and they all contained a middle petroleum distillate, including my control sample. Pihlaja indicated that some glues used in the manufacturing of carpets contain a middle petroleum distillate.

INTERVIEWS

On December 22, 1993, I spoke with ██████████████, who stated the following:

- Upon arriving at the scene, he observed no visible smoke.
- He entered through the back door and saw the victim on the floor.
- There was no visible fire and very little smoke.
- The coffee can on the stove was bubbling.
- The right rear stove burner and oven were on and he could not turn the stove knobs, so the power was turned off in the basement.
- He secured the scene until the sheriff's deputies arrived.

Interviews of the reporting party and the owner's family had been taken by sheriff's deputies. Copies of the interviews are included with their reports.

4

File

CONCLUSION

At this time, it is my opinion that this fire was accidental in nature. I believe that the owner decided to bake after arriving home. While waiting for the items in the oven to finish baking, she went to bed to read a book. While reading, she became aware of a problem in the kitchen. Upon her investigation, she discovered a can of grease on the stove bubbling. While trying to move the can, she caught her clothing on fire. She suffered a heart attack while trying to extinguish the fire.

On December 23, 1993, I was informed by Deputy ████████ that the autopsy had been completed and that the cause of death was a heart attack. He also stated that her carbon monoxide level was at 4%, which was consistent with the cause of death.

At this time, I cannot explain how the paint thinner and the personal papers got into the trash container. The surviving family members could offer no explanation either. The insurance company's investigator will also be submitting samples of the kitchen floor for chemical analysis. The results will be submitted as they become available.

This report will close this file.

Respectfully submitted,

████████████

Deputy State Fire Marshal - Investigator

5

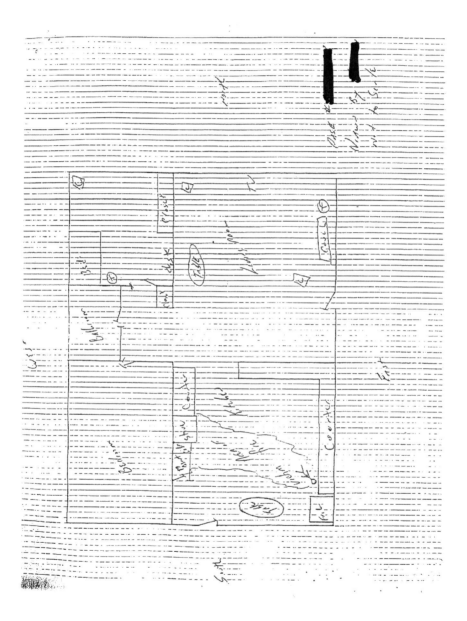

███████ COUNTY LAW ENFORCEMENT CENTER
SUPPLEMENTAL REPORT

PAGE 1   CASE NO: ████████
==
COMPLAINANT: ████████ COUNTY SHERIFF'S DEPARTMENT
==
OFFENSE: FATAL HOUSE FIRE   DATE: 12-22-93
==

The date on this is 12-22-93. The time is 1904 hours. This is Deputy
████████ and I'm at the residence of the fire that took place on County
██████. At this time, Deputy ██████ and myself along with people from Krause
Lock Company are securing the scene. In checking over the premises, this
officer and Deputy ██████ have noticed a couple of items that should be added
to the report.

1. With the power off and the kitchen area completely dark, both
   officers noticed that there is definitely a grease type splatter
   on the two cupboard doors that are on the lower portion of the
   cabinet closest to the refrigerator. These doors in proximity
   to where the victim died would be almost directly above her
   head. Also on the door closest to the refrigerator it is quite
   easy to see that there is a considerable amount of blood splattering
   on that door and following that pattern upward to both doors and up
   to the counter top where the victim attempted to grab the ice cube
   tray separator and also left her fingerprints on the counter top.
   It should also be noted that it appears as if there is blood
   underneath the lip of the counter top. This would have to be
   verified in the daylight, but quite obviously it is unusual that
   blood could reach underneath the counter top unless the victim hit
   quite hard and blood spattered up underneath. Further, on the
   two drawers it should be noted that again in the light of the
   flashlight it appears that there are fingerprints running diagonally
   down as if the victim placed both hands on the counter and they
   slipped off as she was trying to gain a hold to keep herself from
   going to the floor. This pattern extends down to the lower door
   underneath the sink. It should be noted that for a reference
   point that this is the door that ████████████ said that he also
   found a blood splatter on.

2. Further, in case it was not noted in any of the other reports,
   looking closely at the floor, there are two different types of
   material here, one being a shear type material, very lightweight,
   and the other being a heavier material impossible at this time
   to determine what it is but these appear to be melted into the
   carpeting.

End to date. Investigation to continue. Copies to Investigators ████████
and ██████ and also to ████████

==
INVESTIGATING OFFICER: DEPUTY ████████   REPORT BY: DEPUTY ████████
TRANSCRIBED BY: ████   DATE: 12-23-93

```
                    ████████ COUNTY LAW ENFORCEMENT CENTER
                       SUPPLEMENTARY REPORT
 MN0180000                                        CASE NR: ████████
```

| Complainant: ████████ - Sheriff's Investigator |
| County Sheriff's Department |

| Offense: Death Investigation |

Page Nr: 1 of 2   Date: 6/4/94

SYNOPSIS
   The following report contains supplemental information relating to
   the death of Pearl ████████ ████████ provided information in
   relation to this incident. She was a neighbor of Peal ████████
   and believed she observed people at the residence. See details
   section.

   Subject: ████████ ████████
               ████████ ████████

               ████████, Mn. ████████

   Details: 6/4/94 at 1105hrs. Deputy ████████ met with ████████
   at the Law Enforcement Center. She explained that she was Pearl
   ████████ neighbor and had information relating to her death.

   She explained that she used to live in ████████ and has had
   problems with her ex-husband, ████████. They jointly own the
   ████████ was in ████████ and there has been disagreements
   about the financial arrangements. She said that she has had civil
   suits against him. She explained that ████████ has put his
   assets in a friend's name and that he owns nothing. This was done
   to prevent her from obtaining the money. His friend is ████████
   ████████.

   ████████ related that she had her car fixed at ████ Ford and
   it was in good repair. She went to ████████ on October 31, 1993
   and stayed at a friend's house. Her car was tampered with while
   she was there and she believes her ex-husband did it.

   ████████ also talked about her belief that her ex-husband was
   conducting illegal activity at the car wash and that some of the
   financial arrangements were suspicious. Her ex-husband's banker
   is ████████. She believed that he was convicted of arson and
   that the arson was done to burn records of loans to ████████.
   She also believes that her ex-husband was selling stolen property
   at the car wash and that he has a stolen 7mm rifle.

   ████████ related that she works as a nurse at ████████
   Hospital and at ████████ Clinic. She was working in
   ████████ on the nights of December 19th and 21st. She got off
   work at 11:30pm and was home by 12:30am. When she got home she
   would do chores in the barn. She was not sure if it was on the
   19th or 21st but on one of these nights she saw men at Pearl's
   house. She was standing by her barn with the lights on and she
   saw Pearl's house through the woods. There were lights on outside
   of Pearl's also. She saw two figures and heard two male voices.

 INVESTIGATING OFFICER(S):
 REPORT MADE BY:
```
```

CROW WING COUNTY LAW ENFORCEMENT CENTER
SUPPLEMENTARY REPORT

MNO180000   CASE NR: ███████

Complainant: ███████ - Sheriff's Investigator
                      ████ County Sheriff's Department

Offense: Death Investigation

Page Nr: 2 of 2   Date: 6/4/94
She believed one guy was upset. One guy came out and slammed the
door. The car was parked in back of the house and they turned it
on. It was a light gray car with a long nose, like a cougar. The
car left and went North.

        ██████████ said that she did not remember any of this until
recently. She blocked out the incident and it was just coming
back to her in the past few weeks.

        ██████████ believed that her ex-husband may have had somebody
come to the area to kill her. She believed they came her but went
to the wrong house. Her ex-husband did not know *exactly where she
lived* and they went to the wrong house. When asked ████████
said that her ex-husband has never made any overt threats to her
or has assaulted her.

Conclusion: End to date.

INVESTIGATING OFFICER(S):
REPORT MADE BY: Larson   DATE: 6/4/94

```
                CROW WING COUNTY LAW ENFORCEMENT CENTER
                        SUPPLEMENTARY REPORT
  MN0180000
                                                CASE NR: ████████
  Complainant: ████████████ - Sheriff's Investigator
               ██████████ County Sheriff's Department
  Offense: Death Investigation
```

Page Nr: 1 of 1   Date: 10/19/94

SYNOPSIS
The following report contains supplemental information relating to
the death of Pearl ████████████. ████████████ contacted Deputy ████████
with additional information. See details section.

Details: 10/19/94 at 1130hrs. Deputy ████████ talked with ████
████████. She related that ████████████ II is ████████████ son
and she felt that he was one of the people at Pearl's house that
night. She believed that ████ had turned him against her and he
came to do this to her. She did not recognize him but just feels
it was him. She also believes that he was just looking for
records.

████████████ related that she did not remember this information
previously and it just came back to her.

Conclusion: End to date.

INVESTIGATING OFFICER(S):
REPORT MADE BY: ████████

STATE FIRE MARSHAL DIVISION
FIRE INVESTIGATION
EVIDENCE/PHOTO LOG

Date/Time: 12-22-93 + 08:52 Owner/Occupant: Pearl ███████████

Address: ███████████████   City: ██████████████

Investigator: ████████████   Case#: ███████████

Evidence/ Photo	Description	Location:	Found by:
1-4	Exterior Views		
5-7	Views of Ceiling		
8-32	Views of Kitchen		
23-47	Views of Victim		
48-52	Views of Counter by Victim		
53-54	Area of trash Container		
55-57	Close up of Stove		

MINNESOTA DEPARTMENT OF PUBLIC SAFETY
Bureau of Criminal Apprehension
Forensic Science Laboratory
1246 University Avenue
St Paul, MN 55104 Telephone: (612) 642-0700
TDD: (612) 297-2100

Agency Case Number

Laboratory)

LABORATORY ANALYSIS REQUEST

Page 1

TYPE OF CASE: Fire Investigation

AGENCY: State Fire Marshal
COUNTY:

OFFICIAL:
TELEPHONE

ADDITIONAL AGENCIES
County S.O.

ATTENTION:

SECTIONS INVOLVED: CT

CIRCUMSTANCES AND PURPOSE OF ANALYSIS:

Test for paint thinner; house fire

PRINCIPALS: Name -

DOB - Age - Sex - Type - Race

, Pearl

/ /   F   0
/ /   L

Your agency will be notified if the BCA Forensic Science Laboratories
cannot provide a report on this case by <u>January 23, 1994.</u>

ITEM DESCRIPTION OF EVIDENCE:

STORAGE LOCATIO

01   One sealed metal gallon can said to contain debris from the waste basket
      in the kitchen.

02   One sealed metal gallon can said to contain debris from the waste basket
      in the kitchen.

03   One sealed metal gallon can said to contain carpet by stove.

04   One sealed metal gallon can said to contain carpet by stove.

05   One sealed metal quart can said to contain carpet from by the back door.

06   One sealed glass jar said to contain liquid removed from a paint thinner can
      in the basement.

FORENSIC SCIENCE LABORATORY REPORT

The following evidence was received by the Laboratory on December 23, 1993,

from ███████████

Item 06:

One sealed glass jar said to contain liquid removed from a paint thinner can in the

basement.

The following evidence was received by the Laboratory on January 7, 1994,

from ███████████

Item 07:

One sealed metal gallon can said to contain carpet and cloth from near the stove in

kitchen.

RESULTS OF EXAMINATIONS

Examination of the contents of items 7 found it to contain a medium petroleum

distillate such as mineral spirits or the liquid submitted as Item 6.

Interesting to note that not one sample contained grease from the can of grease on

the stove.

FORENSIC SCIENCE LABORATORY
Bureau of Criminal Apprehension
1246 University Avenue
St. Paul, Minnesota 55104-4197
612/642-0700   FAX 612/643-3018   TDD 612/297-2100

December 28, 1993

To:

State Fire Marshal
285 Bigelow Building
450 No. Syndicate St.
St. Paul, MN 55104

Attention: ███████████

The accompanying pages are a report on results of examinations conducted by the Bureau of Criminal Apprehension Forensic Science Laboratory.

This top sheet is only an address page and is not part of the official report.

If you have questions about the report, please contact the BCA Forensic Science Laboratory.

RECEIVED

JAN 1 2 1994

Fire Marshal Division
St. Paul, MN

FORENSIC SCIENCE LABORATORY
Bureau of Criminal Apprehension
1246 University Avenue
St. Paul, Minnesota 55104-4197
612/642-0700   FAX 612/643-3018   TDD 612/297-2100

December 28, 1993

To: ▮▮▮▮, Sheriff
▮▮▮▮ County S.O.
Law Enforcement Center

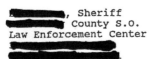

Attention: ▮▮▮▮▮▮

The accompanying pages are a report on results of examinations
conducted by the Bureau of Criminal Apprehension Forensic Science
Laboratory.

This top sheet is only an address page and is not part of the
official report.

If you have questions about the report, please contact the BCA
Forensic Science Laboratory.

FORENSIC SCIENCE LABORATORY REPORT

LABORATORY CASE: ████████

December 28, 1993

EVIDENCE AND SOURCE

The following evidence was received by the Laboratory on December 23, 1993, from ████████

Item 01:
One sealed metal gallon can said to contain debris from the waste basket in the kitchen.

Item 02:
One sealed metal gallon can said to contain debris from the waste basket in the kitchen.

Item 03:
One sealed metal gallon can said to contain carpet by stove.

Item 04:
One sealed metal gallon can said to contain carpet by stove.

Item 05:
One sealed metal quart can said to contain carpet from by the back door.

Item 06:
One sealed glass jar said to contain liquid removed from a paint thinner can in the basement.

Page 2 of 3 Pages

FORENSIC SCIENCE LABORATORY REPORT

LABORATORY CASE: ████████   December 28,1993

RESULTS OF EXAMINATIONS

The liquid submitted as Item 6 was identified as a medium petroleum distillat consistent with mineral spirits or paint thinner.

Examination of the contents of Items 1 through 5 found them all to contain a medium petroleum distillate such as mineral spirits or the liquid submitted as Item 6.

I hereby certify that the above report is true and accurate.

Forensic Scientist III

DISPOSITION OF EVIDENCE:

Please pick up evidence within 30 days after receipt of this report.

DISTRIBUTION: State Fire Marshal - 2; Lab - 1

Page 3 of 3 Pages

Department of Public Safety
Fire Marshal Division
285 Bigelow Building
450 North Syndicate Street
St. Paul, MN 55104

File No. ▆▆▆▆▆

S U P P L E M E N T A L   R E P O R T

Occupant: Pearl ▆▆▆▆▆▆▆

Address: ▆▆▆▆▆▆▆▆

City: ▆▆▆▆   County: ▆▆▆▆▆▆▆

Owner: Pearl ▆▆▆▆▆▆▆

Date and time of fire: December 22, 1993 at 0852 hours

INVESTIGATION REPORT:

On January 12, 1994, I traveled to ▆▆▆▆▆▆ and met with Insurance Investigator ▆▆▆▆▆▆▆ at the fire scene. Additional samples were taken in the kitchen for analysis. Also taken was a carpet sample from the basement. All samples were submitted to a private testing lab by ▆▆▆▆▆.

On January 18, 1994, I spoke with Investigator ▆▆▆▆▆. I was informed that his samples had also tested positive, containing a middle petroleum distillate. The sample from the basement had also tested positive. It was his opinion that the glue in the carpet was causing the positive result.

Respectfully submitted,

▆▆▆▆▆▆

Deputy State Fire Marshal-Investigator
Dated: February 15, 1994

DISPOSITION: CLOSED

1

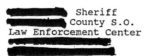

FORENSIC SCIENCE LABORATORY
Bureau of Criminal Apprehension
1246 University Avenue
St. Paul, Minnesota 55104-4197
612/642-0700   FAX 612/643-3018   TDD 612/297-2100

January 25, 1994

To: ███████ Sheriff
    ███████ County S.O.
    Law Enforcement Center
    ███████████████

Attention: ████████████

The accompanying pages are a report on results of examinations conducted by the Bureau of Criminal Apprehension Forensic Science Laboratory.

This top sheet is only an address page and is not part of the official report.

If you have questions about the report, please contact the BCA Forensic Science Laboratory.

FORENSIC SCIENCE LABORATORY
Bureau of Criminal Apprehension
1246 University Avenue
St. Paul, Minnesota 55104-4197
612/642-0700   FAX 612/643-3018   TDD 612/297-2100

January 25, 1994

To:

State Fire Marshal
285 Bigelow Building
450 No. Syndicate St.
St. Paul, MN 55104

Attention: ██████████

The accompanying pages are a report on results of examinations conducted by the Bureau of Criminal Apprehension Forensic Science Laboratory.

This top sheet is only an address page and is not part of the official report.

If you have questions about the report, please contact the BCA Forensic Science Laboratory.

RECEIVED

JAN 3 1 1994

Fire Marshal Division
St. Paul, MN

FORENSIC SCIENCE LABORATORY
Bureau of Criminal Apprehension
1246 University Avenue
St. Paul, Minnesota 55104-4197
612/642-0700   FAX 612/643-3018   TDD 612/297-2100

January 25, 1994

SUPPLEMENTAL REPORT 1 ON THE EXAMINATION OF PHYSICAL EVIDENCE

This report of the BCA Forensic Science Laboratory gives the results of examinations conducted on evidence received from your office.

If court testimony is required, please notify the Forensic Science Laboratory at least two weeks in advance.

LABORATORY DIRECTOR

Forensic Science Supervisor

LABORATORY CASE:	
AGENCY CASE:	
COUNTY:	
REQUESTING AGENCY:	State Fire Marshal
TYPE OF CASE:	Fire Investigation
PRINCIPAL(S):	Pearl

Page 1 of 3 Pages

FORENSIC SCIENCE LABORATORY REPORT

LABORATORY CASE: ███████████   January 25, 1994

EVIDENCE AND SOURCE

The following evidence was received by the Laboratory on December 23, 1993, from ███████████

Item 06:
One sealed glass jar said to contain liquid removed from a paint thinner can in the basement.

The following evidence was received by the Laboratory on January 7, 1994, from ███████████

Item 07:
One sealed metal gallon can said to contain carpet and cloth from near the stove in the kitchen.

Page 2 of 3 Pages

FORENSIC SCIENCE LABORATORY REPORT

LABORATORY CASE: ███████████   January 25, 1994

RESULTS OF EXAMINATIONS

Examination of the contents of Item 7 found it to contain a medium petroleum distillate such as mineral spirits or the liquid submitted as Item 6.

I hereby certify that the above report is true and accurate.

_____

Forensic Scientist III

DISPOSITION OF EVIDENCE:

Please pick up evidence within 30 days after receipt of this report.

DISTRIBUTION: State Fire Marshal - 2; Lab - 1

███████

Page 3 of 3 Pages

Department of Public Safety
Fire Marshal Division
285 Bigelow Building
450 North Syndicate Street
St. Paul, Minnesota 55104

 COPY

File No. ▪▪▪▪▪▪▪▪

Occupant(s):	
PEARL ▪▪▪▪▪▪▪▪▪▪▪	
Address: ▪▪▪▪▪▪▪▪▪▪	Phone: ( ) -
City: ▪▪▪▪▪	County: ▪▪▪▪▪▪▪▪

Owner Name: PEARL ▪▪▪▪▪▪▪▪▪▪▪

Owner Address: ▪▪▪▪▪▪▪▪▪▪▪   Phone:( ) -

     City: ▪▪▪▪▪   State: MINNESOTA   Zip:

Type of occupancy: HOUSE

Approximate Loss: $25,000

Requesting agency: SHERIFF'S OFFICE

Date and time of fire: 12/22/93   0852 Hours

Date and time of request: 12/22/93   0930 Hours

Initial fire department: ▪▪▪▪▪▪▪   FDID:

Fire offical contacted: ▪▪▪▪▪▪▪▪

      BCA contact: N/A   Date:

Cooperating agency(s): SHERIFF'S DEPUTIES ▪▪▪▪▪▪▪▪▪▪▪

       Fire Cause: ACCIDENTAL

Synopsis: THE OWNER/VICTIM WAS TRYING TO REMOVE A CAN OF HOT GREASE FROM ON TOP OF THE STOVE AND HER CLOTHING CAUGHT FIRE.

      Completed by: ▪▪▪▪▪▪▪▪▪▪   Date: 01/27/94

      Disposition: CLOSED

 **APPLIED TECHNICAL SERVICES, INCORPORATED**

1190 Atlanta Industrial Drive, Marietta, Georgia 30066 • (404)423-1400

CERTIFIED TEST REPORT

Ref. ▊▊▊	Date February 4, 1994	Page 1 of 2

Purchase Order #: Verbal - ▊▊▊

▊▊▊▊▊▊
▊▊▊▊▊▊▊▊

<u>Subject:</u>

Claim #   ▊▊▊
File #   ▊▊▊
Insured: Pearl ▊▊▊
Date of Loss: 12-23-93
Analysis of Fire Evidence.

<u>Background</u>

On February 1, 1994, ▊▊▊▊ of ATS received from ▊▊▊▊▊ via UPS the following:

Item 1. One quart can containing burned carpet and underlayment identified as removed from in front of the gas cook stove in the kitchen.

Item 2. One gallon can containing burned carpet identified as removed from below the south kitchen window on the floor.

Item 3. One gallon can containing an unburned carpet sample identified as removed from inside the kitchen entry closet.

Item 4. One quart can containing an unburned carpet sample identified as removed from the basement.

ATS was requested to analyze the samples to check for the presence of ignitable liquid residues.

Prepared by ▊▊▊▊▊▊▊

Reviewed by ▊▊▊▊▊▊▊

My Commission Expires ▊▊▊

Note: Negative samples will be discarded after
30 days unless written instructions to the
contrary are received.

 **APPLIED TECHNICAL SERVICES, INCORPORATED**

1190 Atlanta Industrial Drive, Marietta, Georgia 30066 • (404)423-1400

CERTIFIED TEST REPORT

| Ref. ▬▬▬ | Date February 4, 1994 | Page 2 of 2 |

Test Methods and Results

The samples was/were separated per ASTM Practices E 1412-91 and analyzed per ASTM Method E 1387-90.

Gas chromatographic/mass spectrometric (GC/MS) analysis of concentrated headspace vapors from Items 1, 2, 3 & 4 reveals that each contains components having retention times and mass spectra characteristic of components of known mineral spirits.

All four samples had approximately the same concentration of mineral spirits, with the comparison samples (Items 3 and 4) exhibiting a somewhat lower average molecular weight, presumably due to less exposure to heat.

No determination could be made as to the source of the mineral spirits, but it may have been used as a solvent for the adhesive used to glue to the carpet to the padding.

County Attorney's Office
Courthouse

TELEPHONE
FAX

August 18, 1997

Dear

Enclosed is a copy of the letter our office sent to the Crow Wing County Sheriff,
Sorry it took so long to get to you.

Very truly yours,

County Attorney

.lnc

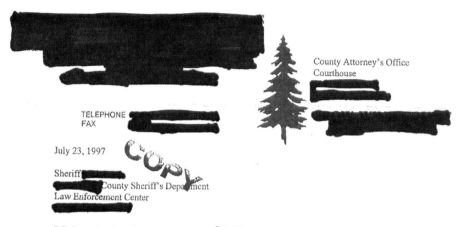

County Attorney's Office
Courthouse

TELEPHONE
FAX

July 23, 1997

Sheriff ▮▮▮▮▮
▮▮▮▮ County Sheriff's Department
Law Enforcement Center
▮▮▮▮▮▮▮

RE: Investigation into the death of Pear▮▮▮▮▮▮▮

Dear Investigator ▮▮▮

▮▮▮▮▮ was in my office this week with information regarding the above-entitled matter. I advised her that I would let your department know that she is in possession of these materials and should you wish her to bring those materials in, or should you wish to speak with her regarding this matter, her address is: ▮▮▮▮▮▮▮▮▮▮▮▮▮▮▮▮▮▮

Should you have any questions or concerns please feel free to contact me at any time.

Very truly yours,

▮▮▮▮▮▮ County Attorney

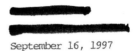

September 16, 1997

County Attorney

Dear

Thank you for forwarding to me a copy of the letter you sent
County Sheriff ■■■■■■, on July 23,1997. I have been unsuccessful in
getting an appointment with Sheriff ■■■■. Mr. ■■■ did return one of my
calls and said he would get back to me. That was weeks ago and I do not
feel the sherrif,s Department is interested in the Pearl ■■■■■■ case.

What more information do you need to re-open the case? You had a body.
You have a very reliable witness. You also have the motive for the murder.
There is also a description of the car and the two males who were seen at
Pearl,s home at 0015 on the night of the murder. I would be available to
fill you in on more information concerning Pearl,s death. Let me tell you
what occurred that night. I can still be reached at, ■■■■■■■■■■■■
■■■■■■■■■■■■■

                                    Sincerely yours,

STATE OF MINNESOTA   DISTRICT COURT

COUNTY OF ██████████   ████ JUDICIAL DISTRICT

****

██████████ County Coroner's Office

CORONER'S INQUEST:

Re: Death of Pearl ██████████

Date of Birth: December 4, 1908

Date of Death: Found December 22, 1993   File No.: ████████

****

BACKGROUND: The death of Pearl ██████████ was originally investigated by the then ████ ██████ County Coroner, Dr. ████████████, who certified the cause of death; the ████████ County Sheriff's Office; the Minnesota State Fire Marshall's Office; ████ Ambulance Service; the ████████ Fire Department; and the Ramsey County Medical Examiner's Office after her body was found in her home following a house fire on December 22, 1993. The house was located on ██████████ and had a rural fire number of ████, in ████████ County.

As a result of the investigation, a death certificate was filed, listing the manner of death as accidental and the cause of death as probable fatal cardiac arrhythmia resulting from thermal injuries. "House Fire" was listed in the section of how injury occurred.

Dr. ████████████ retired as ████████████ Coroner on December 31, 1998, and his records were transferred to the offices of Midwest Forensic Pathology of Anoka, Minnesota, at the direction of the ████████ County Attorney.

1

In January, 2000, Kenneth ██████, an attorney, on behalf of ████████ a neighbor of Pearl ████████ at the time of the death, contacted the ████████ County Attorney's Office with concerns and offered newly recollected and previously unknown information about Mrs. ████████ death.

██████, the ████████ County Attorney, met with Mr. ████████ and was in turn referred to Dr. ████████, the ████████ County Coroner.

The information was reviewed, and following consultation with the County Attorney, the ████████ County Coroner decided to convene an inquest.

PROCEDURE: Dr. ████████, ████████ County Coroner, asked ████████, M.D., J.D., Hennepin County Medical Examiner, to be the Presiding Officer at the inquest. Dr. ████ was appointed Assistant ████████ County Coroner *pro hac vice* for this purpose.

PART I: The inquest was initially convened on May 1, 2001 at the ████████ County Courthouse. Present were Dr. ████████, ████████ County Attorney; Dr. ████████ and ████████, Assistant County Attorney, ████████ County.

WITNESSES AT THE FIRST SESSION:

1) ████████, Fire Investigator, Minnesota Fire Marshal's Office;

2

2) ██████████, Investigator, ████████ County Sheriff's Office; and

3) ████████████, neighbor.

CONCLUSIONS AND DISCUSSION: The testimony of ████████████ and ████████████ clarified and restated the details of the death scene investigation. Photographs of the death scene were introduced, including several showing views of the kitchen of the home which had extensive fire damage. The Deputy Sheriff and Fire Marshal gave testimony consistent with initial reports. Both witnesses amplified details, and their recollections were entirely consistent with the death scene, descriptions, death scene photographs, autopsy photographs, and physical findings made at autopsy.

██████████ testimony was lengthy, complex, and required substantial background explanation as part of the questioning. Ms. ████████ was a cooperative and obviously sincere witness. The delivery and narration of her testimony were fundamentally persuasive. After careful scrutiny, however, it is concluded that her testimony contained numerous details strongly inconsistent with the death scene investigation and the autopsy findings. Dr. ████████ and Dr. ████████ therefore did not find this testimony to be credible.

To supplement the testimony and exhibits offered at the inquest, Dr. ████████ and Dr. ████████ were driven to the roadway adjacent to the decedent's residence and Ms. ████████ former residence, and from the roadway inspected the general terrain

3

and surroundings. Although it was springtime and there was more foliage than when the decedent died in winter, it was clear from this inspection that Ms. ███████ recollection of the events was neither plausible nor possible.

Ms. ███████ who had lived adjacent to the decedent, based her testimony on a lately recovered memory that two acquaintances of her then-estranged husband had caused the decedent's death and the fire at the decedent's home, apparently having mistaken the decedent's home for Ms. ███████ These recollections do not correlate with the distance between the place where Ms. ███████ says she was standing, the location of the decedent's home and the intervening terrain.

PART II: On July 25, 2001, the inquest was reconvened, this time at the Ramsey County Medical Examiner's Office, in order to take the testimony of Dr. ███████████, the Ramsey County Medical Examiner, who performed the autopsy in this case.

WITNESSES:

Dr. ███████████

CONCLUSIONS AND DISCUSSION: Dr. ███████ confirmed all of the autopsy findings and discounted any significant physical injury other than thermal injury. He stated that the petechial hemorrhages described in the sclerae of the eyes, and bloodstaining in the neck, were artifactual. He further confirmed that these observations were noted, but

4

were not enumerated as findings in the autopsy report because he had concluded after completing the autopsy that they were not the result of disease or injury and were not significant. The photographs of the death scene and the body were reviewed by Dr. ████. Several photographs clearly indicated that the decedent was alive after the fire started; markings in soot documented her struggles during the fire.

Dr. ████ concluded that the fire was caused by grease on a heated stove burner. He concluded that the grease caught fire, and that the decedent died while futilely attempting to put out the fire. These conclusions are supported by all of the data and interpretations by expert investigators who saw things firsthand.

FURTHER DISCUSSION: Despite its obvious sincerity and fundamental persuasiveness, it is the finding of this inquest that ████████ recollections of events, "recovered" for the first time four years after the death, are incorrect. Her recollections are refuted by the tangible evidence in this case and are at odds with the logical conclusions to which that evidence leads.

At the time of Mrs. ████████ death, Ms. ████████ had no immediate recollection indicating that the death was anything but a tragic accident. Ms. ████████ new testimony about the night of Pearl ████████ death illustrates a phenomenon ("recovered memory") that has not stood up to scientific scrutiny. Without debating that issue, however, the failure of her recollections to correlate with the physical and historical facts of this case is the reason for rejecting them.

5

FINAL CONCLUSIONS: No significant discrepancies were found in the investigation or in the conclusions drawn by Dr. ███████ and Dr. ██████ It is the determination of this inquest that the cause and manner of death remain as originally certified.

████████████████████, M.D., J.D.
Chief Presiding Officer
Assistant ████████ County Coroner

██████████ County Coroner

6

November 6, 2001

, County Attorney

RE: File No: ██████
    Death of Pearl ██████

Dear ██████

My attorney, Kenneth ██████, recently sent me a copy of the Corner's Inquest. Is it possible for me to receive a copy of the reports from the witnesses at the first session, ██████ and ██████

I would like to appeal the decision of the Coroner's Inquest. It was based on facts that are incorrect and assumed. There are several important facts at issue.

I believe it is very crucial to have an on site inspection, but it should have been with the witness, ██████. The scene can not be inspected from the roadway. The woods are very thick at the roadway and it is approximately 300 feet from the site where the witness stood, which is fairly clear of trees. There is old farm machinery in this once cleared area, further more there is now almost 8 years of growth in the area. My witnesses have clearly seen the house from where I stood, and in the summer of 1994.

My recollection of events did not take place 4 years later. I went to ██████ in the summer of 1994 to report what I saw, only 6 months after the occurrence. This can be substantiated in the Sheriff's report.

Dr. ██████ states that petechial hemorrhages described in the sclerae of the eyes, and bloodstaining in the neck were artifactual, and not the result of disease or injury. In the next paragraph he states the decedent died while attempting to put out the fire. Sounds like a contradiction to me. Petechial hemorrhages are caused from extreme prostration, and could have been inflicted by an intruder, as well as the bloodstaining. I could hear the arguing in the house. I did not hear Pearl ██████ scream as she would have if she were alive when she was set afire.

Directing your attention to the can of grease on the stove, which is probably bacon fat or animal fat. Must have been a very large can as to have spilled on the victim, carpet and into the papers in the bag. I can't believe the samples sent to forensic labs could not have detected the presence of grease, instead called the substance mineral spirits.

I have taken the trouble to list a few facts at issue.
1. Was the victim alive before the fire, carbon monoxide in the lungs rules that out.
2. Accelerant paint thinner, grease, or mineral spirits.
3. Position of the Witness and the view of the scene.
4. Artifactual- petechial hemorrhage or blood staining-good evidence of strangulation?
5. Why were documents put in a bag, and who put them there?
6. Did the ███████ Sheriff's Department do a thorough investigation, and interview the neighbors? They did not! I was a neighbor
7. How thorough was the Fire marshall in his report?
8. Were expert homicide detectives involved in the case?
9. Marks in the soot on the floor, by whom?
10. Disputed time of recall.

If, ███████ would have done his job and interviewed the neighbor, mainly██ ██████, the outcome would have been so different. He would have found a neighbor who was frightened and crying, who would have told him "it was suppose to have been me." That morning of Pearl's death, I still remembered seeing two guys over at Pearl's after I got home from work at midnight, and would have passed that information on.

Please be kind enough to assist me with advice as to what I can do to have this reconsidered. I am told by my attorney that spontaneous recollection is one of the most effective proofs of an evaluation.. Perhaps I should have followed my first instinct and gone for hypnosis or a lie detector tests, and I will.

Sincerely yours,

███████

cc: Dr. ███████
    Kenneth ███████

166

COUNTY ATTORNEY'S OFFICE
COUNTY SERVICE BUILDING

TELEPHONE
FAX

November 16, 2001

Re: Death of Pearl

Dear

I am in receipt of, and have reviewed, your November 6, 2001 letter concerning the above. I am also in receipt of the final Order arising out of the Coroner's Inquest surrounding Ms. ████████ death. I have reviewed the final report and filed the same with ████████████ District Court. I have also filed copies of the transcripts of the Coroner's Inquest proceedings with the ████████ County Court Administrator's Office. If you wish to acquire copies of any of these documents, it would be necessary for you to make arrangements through the ████████ County Court Administrator's Office for the same. I do advise you that there may be a cost associated with any such request. The amount that may be involved is something you would need to discuss with the Court Administrator's Office.

From the tone of your letter, it is my impression that you disagree with the Coroner's Inquest result. However, I consider this matter concluded and have consequently closed my file. Therefore, the ████████ County Attorney's Office will have no further involvement in this matter.

Very truly yours,

County Attorney

cc: Dr.

167

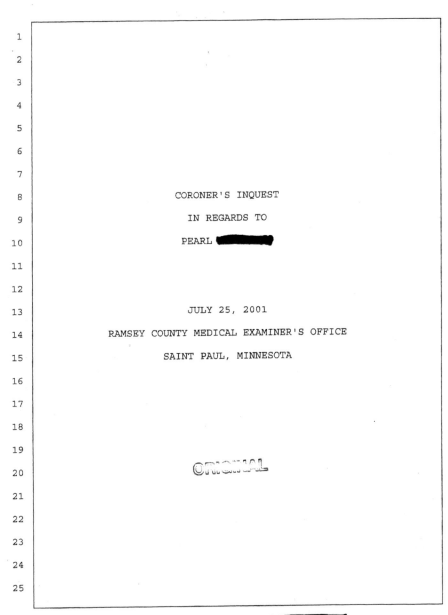

```
 1
 2
 3
 4
 5
 6
 7
 8                    CORONER'S INQUEST
 9                     IN REGARDS TO
10                     PEARL ███████
11
12
13                     JULY 25, 2001
14        RAMSEY COUNTY MEDICAL EXAMINER'S OFFICE
15               SAINT PAUL, MINNESOTA
16
17
18
19
20                      ORIGINAL
21
22
23
24
25
```

SHADDIX & ASSOCIATES ███████

```
 1
 2      APPEARANCES:
 3      ██████████████████.
                        County Attorney
 4      County Service Building
 5      ███████████████████████
        ██████████████████
 6      ████████████████, M.D., J.D.
        Presiding Officer of Inquest
 7      Chief Hennepin County Medical Examiner
        530 Chicago Avenue
 8      Minneapolis, Minnesota  55415
 9      ███████████████, M.D.
        ████████████ County Coroner
10      Midwest Forensic Pathology
        3960 Coon Rapids Boulevard
11      Coon Rapids, Minnesota  55330
12      ████████████████, M.D.
        Chief Ramsey County Medical Examiner
13      300 East University Avenue
        Saint Paul, Minnesota  55101
14
15
16
17
18
19
20
21
22              (Whereupon, the following proceedings were
23      duly had, and entered of record, to-wit:)
24
25
```

SHADDIX & ASSOCIATES   ██████████████████

169

3

1   DR. ██████: As acting Special ██████

2   County Coroner, I would ask you to swear the witness and

3   that the witness state his name.

4   THE WITNESS: ████████, ██████.

5   ████████, M.D.,

6   having been first duly sworn, was

7   examined and testified on his oath as follows:

8   EXAMINATION

9   BY MR. ██████:

10   Q   Good morning, Dr. ██████. How are you today?

11   A   Very good, sir. How are you?

12   Q   Good. As you know, we're here on a continued coroner's

13   inquest regarding the death of Pearl ████████. We

14   previously had convened up in ████████ back in May, I

15   think, of this year; and there were some questions that

16   came up that the presiding officer wished to ask you

17   concerning the autopsy that you did on Pearl ████████.

18   A   All right.

19   Q   And just before we get going with that, I'm not going to,

20   myself, ask you the questions, I'm going to allow -- the

21   presiding officers will do that. But just for purposes of

22   a record, by the clock on the wall, we are here at the

23   Ramsey County Medical Examiner's Office, and by the clock

24   on the wall in the conference room, we started at

25   approximately 9:31 a.m. Dr. ██████ has taken the stand.

SHADDIX & ASSOCIATES   ████████

4

```
 1                  Doctor, I'm going to show you what's
 2       previously been marked as Inquest Exhibit Number 16 and
 3       ask you to look at that exhibit.
 4   A   I have looked at it.
 5   Q   Do you recognize that, Doctor?
 6   A   I do.  This -- I do recognize it.
 7   Q   What is it?
 8   A   This is a photocopy of the final autopsy protocol, some
 9       laboratory results, hard copy from the lab, as well as a
10       copy of the provisional report produced by this office in
11       conjunction with the examination of Pearl ████████.
12   Q   And that was for her autopsy, correct?
13   A   That's right.
14   Q   And you did the autopsy yourself?
15   A   I did.
16   Q   Doctor, do you have a copy of that with you here today?
17   A   I do.
18   Q   I'm going to give this exhibit back to the presiding
19       officers so they can use it for purposes of their
20       questioning and would ask, if you need to, to please feel
21       free to look at your records and reports in this matter.
22   A   Thank you.
23                  MR. ████  With that, I would turn it over to
24       the presiding officer to continue.
25                       EXAMINATION
```

SHADDIX & ASSOCIATES ████████████

5

```
 1  BY DR. ██████:
 2  Q    Dr. ██████, I'm going to ask some questions preliminarily.
 3       I think Dr. ██████ may supplement what I ask, too; and
 4       we'll try to do this in a formal way, but probably with a
 5       little more informality than you often have in a court or
 6       even a deposition setting, because this is an inquest and
 7       because Dr. ██████ and I and you are all physicians and,
 8       I think, can talk at a medical level and convey and
 9       exchange information probably most efficiently that way.
10  A    All right.
11  Q    So if that's satisfactory with you?
12  A    Sure.
13  Q    And I'm going to start in kind of an inverted way and ask
14       you what your final conclusion was in the case, and then
15       we'll backtrack and go through your process in reaching
16       that conclusion.
17  A    Sure.  It was my impression of -- are you asking for the
18       cause of death?
19  Q    Well, the cause and what you would have assigned as manner
20       of death in this particular case.
21  A    From the autopsy findings, it was my impression that the
22       subject's death was probably due to a fatal cardiac
23       arrhythmia due to thermal injuries that she suffered while
24       in her private residence.
25            The manner of death, as much as I knew at the
```

SHADDIX & ASSOCIATES

6

```
 1         time of the initial investigation was accidental; however,

 2         as in all autopsies, since they are at the beginning of a

 3         death investigation, if we don't feel that the data is

 4         complete, we put down, "Pending investigation," which is

 5         what I did in this case.

 6    Q    I understand.  Now, the date of the examination was on

 7         December 23rd, 1923 (sic), as I understand it, at about

 8         11:00 in the morning?

 9    A    True.

10    Q    So that, really, was very, very shortly after the body had

11         arrived here overnight at -- the date of death was listed

12         as the 22nd, if I'm correct in this, and the body was

13         brought here to this facility, then, during the day or

14         overnight the day before you did the autopsy; is that --

15    A    The body arrived in our office on the morning of

16         December 23rd at 9:40 in the morning and was subsequently

17         autopsied at 11:00 by myself on that same date, yes.

18    Q    And so it was a case that was sent in and you, obviously,

19         would not have had a chance to see the scene at that time?

20    A    True, true.

21    Q    Were scene photographs available to you that --

22    A    Yes.

23    Q    -- had been taken, or video or other --

24    A    Thirty-five millimeter print photographs were made

25         available from the death scene.
```

SHADDIX & ASSOCIATES

1 Q   So you had that benefit. And that would be typical of the

2   approach that this office would use on a referral case of

3   that sort, would be my question to you?

4 A   Yes.

5 Q   And I'm wondering if you could just look at your report

6   and highlight the findings that you discovered during the

7   autopsy, not just the cause of death, but just, basically,

8   go through the things that you encountered.

9 A   Well, basically, Mrs. ██████████, at the time of the exam,

10   was an 86-year-old Caucasian female that measured five

11   feet, three inches in height and weighed 151 pounds.

12   She had evidence of severe thermal injuries

13   on the distal aspects of her upper and lower extremities

14   characterized by second and third degree burns. Some of

15   these exhibited evidence of charring.

16   Associated with these severe injuries was

17   deposition of soot in the mucosa of her nose and mouth, as

18   well as her larynx and the trachea. This was not the

19   dense soot deposition you would expect with someone found

20   in a conflagration of a home where the house is completely

21   burned, but there is presence of soot on the mucosa of

22   these areas. As you get farther down into the airway, it

23   becomes less so that in the mainstem bronchi, soot can be

24   observed, but it's only traces.

25 Q   If I can just interrupt and elaborate with a follow-up

SHADDIX & ASSOCIATES

1		question on that, I'm going to ask your inference from
2		that. Would it be that the soot was deposited there
3		passively, just by the environment that the body was in
4		after death, or that there was actually some actual active
5		inhalation of sooty or burning products of combustion?
6	A	The latter.
7	Q	The latter? So you would conclude that she was alive
8		during the time that the fire was taking place in the
9		residence?
10	A	Yes.
11	Q	Is that a fair characterization of your conclusion?
12	A	Yes.
13	Q	Why don't you go on.
14	A	To confirm the presence of the soot present, a blood
15		carbon monoxide was done, which is low at 4.9 percent; but
16		if I remember right, I don't know if Mrs. ▮▮▮▮▮▮
17		smoked, so that may be of some importance.
18	Q	Let me just give a follow-up question. Make the
19		assumption or hypothetically, if she were a nonsmoker, a
20		woman of her age, would 4.9 be a typical expected carbon
21		monoxide level, or would it be one that would be above or
22		below what one would expect?
23	A	For a nonsmoker in this office, that would be an elevated
24		level.
25	Q	Again, I just would ask, the inference, then, would be,

9

1		again, that there was some active inhalation of products
2		of combustion, it's just that they did not reach what, for
3		you, would be a lethal level, but it does indicate, again,
4		her being alive or suggests that she was alive at the time
5		of the fire or during the fire?
6	A	True.
7	Q	Go on.
8	A	The second finding that we found -- and the thermal
9		injuries and the related were the first set of things that
10		were important. The second thing was, basically,
11		examination of her cardiovascular system, which showed
12		cardiomegaly, or enlargement of the heart, with left
13		ventricular hypertrophy, as well as evidence of advanced
14		coronary vessel disease. We were told by investigators
15		from ▮▮▮▮▮ County at the time that the lady had a
16		previous diagnosis of congestive heart failure. Those
17		were the two principal findings.
18		Toxicology on this lady --
19	Q	I'm just going to jump in for a second before we get to
20		toxicology and elaborate a little bit about the condition
21		of the heart. You said that the heart was enlarged?
22	A	Uh-huh.
23	Q	Can you give me the weight? Did you record the weight?
24	A	Five hundred and seventy grams.
25	Q	I guess, as a physician, you would clearly identify this

SHADDIX & ASSOCIATES ▮▮▮▮▮▮▮▮

1		as an enlarged heart?
2	A	I would.
3	Q	All right. And coronary vessel disease would not be -- it
4		might be average for someone of her age, but would not be
5		insignificant, it would indicate a serious health problem
6		relative to the circulation to the heart muscle; is that
7		correct?
8	A	That is my belief, yes.
9	Q	That is a fair characterization of that, okay. And I
10		would, again, just underscore that there was a clinical
11		history of congestive heart failure. And for the purposes
12		of elaborating, would it be fair to say that that would
13		indicate that the heart had shown an inability to maintain
14		adequate circulation to one degree or another; would that
15		be a fair summarization of that clinical history?
16	A	That would be true.
17	Q	Why don't you go on.
18	A	The additional findings had indicated the lady had some
19		evidence of past cardiovascular. She had some evidence of
20		thickening or hypertrophy of her left ventricular wall at
21		1.8 centimeters, a right ventricular hypertrophy at 0.7
22		and interventricular width of 2.0 centimeters. That taken
23		in part with her cardiomegaly and her previous diagnosis,
24		clinical diagnosis of congestive heart failure, led us to
25		believe that this lady's heart was not normal.

SHADDIX & ASSOCIATES

```
 1                    Her toxicology, the third part, was,
 2        essentially, negative for the presence of alcohol or other
 3        drugs with the exception of acetaminophen, which was found
 4        in her urine, but was at a very low level.
 5   Q    I'll just interrupt and have you elaborate a little bit.
 6        Acetaminophen would be the active ingredient in Tylenol, a
 7        common over-the-counter pain medication?
 8   A    Correct.
 9   Q    And the level would be one that would be seen in urine
10        where someone has used that drug appropriately; would that
11        be a reasonable inference?
12   A    Yes.
13   Q    And I would just ask, is it unusual to detect that as part
14        of a urine screen in your work as a forensic pathologist
15        and medical examiner?
16   A    No, that is commonly seen.
17   Q    And I'll just -- well, let me ask one more question, and
18        that is that I notice that there is a very, very long list
19        of drugs that the gas chromatography eliminated as a
20        possibility and would just ask if it isn't correct that
21        this is a very, very broad array of both drugs of abuse
22        and commonly encountered pharmaceuticals so it's a very
23        comprehensive -- if not a completely comprehensive screen,
24        it's a very elaborate drug screen?
25   A    It is.  That's the way it was intended by our laboratory,
```

12

1		so between examining either the serum or the urine, we're
2		able to, essentially, test for the presence of anywhere
3		from 30 to 50 drugs of common use or abuse.
4	Q	And then I'll just let you go on.
5	A	The rest of the examination in the laboratory consisted of
6		a sexual assault exam, which is done on -- or can be done
7		on cases like this, and was done, and was negative for the
8		presence of seminal fluid or sperm.
9	Q	And I look at those acid phosphatase levels and would also
10		just say that those are values that can be seen in the
11		absence of any sexual activity. The fact that there is a
12		particular numerical value does not necessarily mean that
13		there's male secretion but, rather, these would be in the
14		range that are encountered in death investigation; would
15		that be correct?
16	A	True.
17	Q	I then would just ask if you have any other comments on
18		the examination that you did, anything else that you
19		encountered that was out of the ordinary or --
20	A	To my recollection, no.
21	Q	Then I would move to a couple of places and I'm going to
22		direct your attention to page 4, right at the very, very
23		bottom, the last four lines of page 4 that says, and I'll
24		just read it aloud, "Inspection of the palpebral and
25		bulbar conjunctiva reveal prominent petechial hemorrhages

SHADDIX & ASSOCIATES

13

1   present in the palpebral conjunctiva bilaterally.

2   Ecchymosis can be observed in the bulbar conjunctiva on

3   either side." And it mentions that, "The periorbital soft

4   tissues reveal singeing of --" going over to page 5 --

5   "the eyebrows in the supraorbital regions bilaterally."

6   I'll just maybe have you comment on the

7   significance you gave to that, if you felt that that was

8   artifactual or something that was not pivotal in assessing

9   the case.

10 A   Well, the injuries were noted, and that is why they were

11   described in the autopsy protocol, but taken in the

12   context of the subject's body, I cannot rule out that they

13   are not artifact from the fire and the woman's death,

14   since I was under the impression at the time we did the

15   exam that this lady may have lived, at least for some

16   time, after the fire started, but could see no other

17   injuries present on her body that would be indicative of

18   an assault.

19 Q   Okay. I want to move on to -- it will take me a second to

20   find it here -- page 11 and the neck structures. Rather

21   than go through this, I would just have you read, I guess,

22   the first -- what appears to be the first paragraph. I

23   don't think we need to read about the thyroid gland, but

24   just read that paragraph, your description of the pharynx

25   and the larynx.

14

```
 1  A    You want it read?

 2  Q    Well, you can read it to yourself.  Why don't I read it

 3       aloud.  "The pharynx and larynx are normally developed.

 4       Soft tissue hemorrhage having a burgundy color can be

 5       observed about the left carotid artery and left subclavian

 6       vein.  The thyroid cartilage and cricoid cartilage are

 7       free of fracture."  I may be -- we'll just jump down to

 8       the sentence that says, "Strands of soot-like material can

 9       be observed attached to the mucosa of the epiglottis, as

10       well as about the false and true vocal cords and extending

11       down into the inferior laryngeal compartment and

12       throughout the subject's trachea."  And I would again say

13       that this is recapitulation of what we discussed earlier.

14            Then it says, "Multiple petechial hemorrhages

15       can be observed in the inferior laryngeal cavity measuring

16       1 millimeter or less in size.  The false and true vocal

17       cords are within normal limits, grossly.  The trachea is

18       free of obstruction with an intact, glossy, unremarkable,

19       mucosal surface."

20            I wanted to have you comment on the soft

21       tissue hemorrhage near the left carotid artery and left

22       subclavian vein.  It -- would they indicate some kind of

23       compression or injury?  Would they be consistent with

24       artifact?  I would just ask your --

25  A    Given the way they are described in the autopsy protocol
```

SHADDIX & ASSOCIATES

1   and given my -- the normal operating procedure for

2   describing internal traumatic injuries on the examination

3   of a neck, these are artifactual, in my best opinion.

4   Traumatic injuries, when identified within the neck, are

5   described in another format or are used in another format

6   that is commonly employed in the office.

7   Q   I'm just going to -- I'm hoping not to interrupt your

8   train of thought or answer, but the fact that those are

9   not listed as your -- among your final diagnoses would be

10   a confirmation of your interpretation of those at the time

11   you saw them as being artifactual or insignificant in

12   terms of the analysis of this case; would that be a

13   correct characterization?

14   A   That is true. We do not list -- we do not list, as a

15   normal course, the artifactual findings on the autopsy

16   protocol because of the confusion that sometimes can

17   arise.

18   Further, an examination of her neck showed

19   that the thyroid and cricoid cartilage showed no evidence

20   of fracture, and there was no fracture of the hyoid bone.

21   No associated hemorrhage was noted in the surrounding soft

22   tissues. This is examined for in every case. If this was

23   noted, that would have been described in the autopsy

24   protocol and would be clearly delineated. It was my

25   impression, and from reviewing this, I think this is more

SHADDIX & ASSOCIATES ▬▬▬▬▬▬

16

```
1        likely due to an artifactual area of hemorrhage on the
2        lower neck region.
3   Q    I want to raise another point with you and, certainly, I'm
4        not trying to lead you, but certainly feel free to
5        disagree.  I think, would you agree, that it's true that
6        in cases where heart failure is a cause of death, that
7        there is often quite intense congestion of the upper
8        structures of the body because of failure of the heart to
9        be able to pump properly and that, oftentimes, this does
10       give the chance of artifactual change because of
11       engorgement of blood vessels in the upper part of the
12       body, the upper shoulders and the neck?  Would that be a
13       fair characterization of circumstances in the cases of
14       heart failure?
15  A    That has been our experience, yes.
16  Q    And, again, that would also reconcile with the finding
17       that you saw in the neck in the autopsy, then, and the
18       interpretation that these are artifactual changes?
19  A    That is one explanation, yes.
20  Q    I was going to ask Dr. ██████████ for the photographs here.
21       I think the one I wanted to look -- we can just sort of go
22       off the record here.
23                  (Discussion held off the record.)
24  BY DR. ██████████
25  Q    One of the things I'm going to do, Dr. ██████, I'm just
```

SHADDIX & ASSOCIATES ██████████████

1   going to give you the notebook that has the photographs

2   and have you just flip through these to kind of put you in

3   context to the case and, hopefully, that will --

4   MR. ████ If I can interject at this point,

5   if you're going to refer to any photographs, it would be

6   my recommendation that -- we elected not to individually

7   mark every photograph because of the informal motion, so

8   if you're going to refer to photographs, the envelopes

9   that contain certain sets have a deposition exhibit

10   number, the three-ring binder type of exhibit has a

11   number; so, if you could, refer to --

12   DR. ████████ I will --

13   ████████ -- that specifically in

14   identifying the photographs.

15 BY DR. ████████

16 Q The one that I'm giving you now is Exhibit Number 4. It

17   includes written materials, but I'm directing you to the

18   photographs.

19   Have you had a chance to look at those?

20 A I have.

21 Q And have they helped you recall more about the case or at

22   least been sort of a --

23 A I have not seen all of these photographs. Some of these

24   photographs were provided at the time of the examination

25   performed by this office and do illustrate what we

```
1          previously knew about this case.

2   Q      Very good.  I'm going to show you now another grouping of

3          photographs that comprise Inquest Exhibit Number 8, and

4          they are -- I'm just going to count them here.  There are

5          14 photographs.  I'm going to ask that you keep them in

6          the sequence that they are.

7   A      Okay.

8   Q      I have a couple of questions with respect to some of them.

9   A      I have looked at the photographs provided for Exhibit

10         Number 8.

11  Q      What I'm going to do is I'm going to take the first four

12         photographs from the group and I'm going to characterize

13         them, and you are certainly free to disagree with me, but

14         these, basically, show the body in its original position

15         in the home, and I would ask that you observe those

16         photographs and orient them whichever way you would want.

17  A      All right.

18  Q      And I think it would be correct to say that the body is in

19         a prone position; would that be correct?

20  A      True.

21  Q      At the edge of a countertop?

22  A      True.

23  Q      And that, actually, as one looks at one of the photographs

24         here, one can actually see that it's next to the

25         refrigerator and that there is some somewhat melted object
```

1   that is dripped over the edge of the countertop --

2 A True.

3 Q -- just in front of the body; and one can see, I think you

4   would probably agree, that the floor, for the most part,

5   under the body is somewhat spared with respect to or in

6   contrast to some of the surrounding carpet, indicating

7   that the body lay in this position during the fire. Would

8   you agree with that?

9 A True.

10 Q Next I'm going to show you the fifth and sixth photographs

11   that show the counter more completely next to the area of

12   the refrigerator here and shows some markings made on the

13   countertop and would ask if, in your opinion, the marks

14   would be consistent with the decedent dragging her hand or

15   fingers across the countertop through soot that already

16   existed on the countertop and collapsing to the position

17   shown in the first four photographs?

18 A I thought that that was one possibility, yes.

19 Q I'm going to supplement that, then, with two more

20   photographs that show the stove, show what appear to be

21   some scorched muffins on top of the stove, a melted device

22   which I believe to be a clock that stopped and,

23   unfortunately, is unreadable with respect to its specific

24   time --

25 A Uh-huh.

20

1	Q	-- and a can which, just to characterize some earlier
2		testimony, was felt to contain grease that was present on
3		the countertop.
4	A	Right.
5	Q	And would ask if, in your experience as a medical examiner
6		and a person who has investigated deaths related to fire,
7		whether fire in lard, grease or cooking oil is consistent
8		with a fire of this sort and a death of this sort.
9	A	It has been our experience that open containers containing
10		animal fats or lards, so forth, are extremely flammable
11		and, if left in an open container such as is shown in the
12		photograph, would have a tendency to catch on fire and
13		could explain a sudden fire that appeared to be centered
14		over the range area of the kitchen and surrounding the
15		subject's body as discovered or as shown in the
16		photographs provided.
17	Q	And I just have one other question or one other photograph
18		I was going to show that, again, shows the floor after the
19		body was removed and would ask if it's your opinion that
20		that again confirms that she lay on the floor during the
21		time that the fire was in progress and that shows some
22		sparing of the rug beneath?
23	A	It does, yes.
24		DR. ████ I would ask Dr. ████ if
25		you have any questions.

SHADDIX & ASSOCIATES ████

```
 1              (Discussion held off the record.)

 2              DR. ██████: No, I really don't have any

 3         further questions.

 4   BY DR. ██████

 5   Q   I do have one question suggested by Dr. ██████, and that

 6       was, when we did the first portion of the inquest in May,

 7       we were told that the photographs in this case had -- were

 8       no longer available. I just would ask to have you confirm

 9       or refute that. Are the photographs still unavailable?

10   A   The photographs are unavailable in the office. Their

11       absence in the office -- all of them are absent, which is

12       usually the case, when we used to use 35-millimeter film,

13       if they had been sent out for duplication. We commonly

14       provided this for the people that would reference this.

15       Since they are not here, I must still assume that whoever

16       we released them to to have them duplicated did not return

17       them and we cannot find them, and that is where the matter

18       is at this time.

19   Q   And I would just, at this point, give you the opportunity

20       to add any other information you have, any other thoughts

21       or any other advice or counsel that you would give

22       Dr. ██████ and me, since you are also a medical examiner

23       with respect to this case.

24   A   No further comment.

25   Q   I'll maybe just make one other comment, that there has
```

```
 1        been a witness who came forward who, after a long period
 2        of time, recollected a memory of seeing other individuals
 3        at or near the house that evening.  Is there anything in
 4        your autopsy report or investigation of the case that
 5        would necessitate someone else being involved in or
 6        responsible for or a person who would catalyze a
 7        conflagration in a death of this sort?
 8   A    At the time of the investigation that was performed by the
 9        office, I told the officers at that time and still do
10        believe that the subject's death is due to a home fire
11        and, in all probability, is due to the subject's own
12        actions.  I don't think anybody else is involved.  I
13        didn't think that then; I don't think that now.
14                    DR. ████████:  Thank you very much.
15                    CONTINUED EXAMINATION
16   BY ████████:
17   Q    The only question I might have, if I may, at one point,
18        Dr. ████████, you were questioned about the bottom of page 4,
19        top of page 5 of the autopsy, basically, to use my
20        non-medical layman's terms, some injuries about the face
21        of the victim?
22   A    Uh-huh.
23   Q    Could those types of injuries be consistent with the
24        victim having fallen and striking the countertop and floor
25        to find where the victim was laying?
```

23

```
 1  A      Yes.  I think that would be one possibility -- that's why
 2          I think that is one possibility for the injuries that were
 3          noted to the eyes and may be responsible for one of the
 4          injuries to the subject's neck region.
 5                      MR. ████    Thank you.  I have no other
 6          questions.
 7                      DR. ████████    With that, I would just excuse
 8          you and thank you very much for your cooperation and help
 9          in the matter that we're considering.
10                      THE WITNESS:  Thank you.
11                      DR. ██████:  I declare the inquest, again,
12          closed at this point in time.
13                      MR. ████    For the record, at this point in
14          time I would just note that it is approximately 10:03 a.m.
15          again by the clock on the wall in the conference room as
16          previously noted.
17                      (Short break taken.)
18                      MR. ████    The time is now approximately
19          10:11 a.m., again by the clock on the conference room wall
20          as previously referenced.  We have reconvened the
21          coroner's inquest.  Present in the room are the presiding
22          officers, the court reporter and myself, ████████ County
23          Attorney ████████.
24                      Dr. ██████, I think you have indicated to
25          me off the record that there are some closing comments you
```

SHADDIX & ASSOCIATES   ████████

1   may wish to make or a little more of a record. At that

2   point you believe you may be in a position to conclude

3   this coroner's inquest. I would turn the matter over to

4   you at this time.

5   DR. ███████: Thank you. The first thing

6   I'm going to do is, just in the format of just informally

7   questioning Dr. ███████, verify that on May 16th, as we

8   had concluded or just after we had concluded the first

9   phase of this inquest with Deputy ███████ of the ███

10 ███ County Sheriff's Office, we were taken to the highway

11 area in front of the two homes, ███████ home and

12 the decedent's home, not with the intent of making a

13 direct scene inspection, but with seeing the contour and

14 the basic milieu of the two homes as part of the

15 evaluation of the testimony about the evening of the death

16 and would ask you to verify or refute that we noticed that

17 there is a substantial distance between the two homes and

18 that the distance does correlate with Witness ███████

19 testimony and that, in addition, we noted that there is

20 unevenness of the ground and a convexity to the space

21 between the fence line and the decedent's home and that

22 there is a substantial amount of brush or small tree-like

23 vegetation that, at the time of our observation, had

24 leaves on many of the branches. But our conclusion was

25 that even without leaves it would present virtually a

1   curtain between the two places, the point of observation

2   and the point of -- that was described by the witness. I

3   would ask that you either amplify or verify our

4   conclusions.

5   DR. ██████ Yes, we did have the

6   opportunity to go out and view the scene from the road.

7   We did not enter either of the houses. Both Dr. ██████

8   and I were surprised at the amount of vegetation and feel

9   that even with the absence of leaves in the wintertime, it

10   would have made viewing Pearl ██████ home extremely

11   difficult.

12   DR. ██████ It would almost -- in my

13   opinion, it would almost require x-ray vision, I guess.

14   DR. ██████ Or binoculars, yes.

15   DR. ██████ Or a stepladder or something,

16   a very tall stepladder.

17   DR. ██████ There was quite a hill or

18   convexity between the two properties, and it was very

19   difficult to view the distance between the horse pen and

20   Pearl ██████ home.

21   DR. ██████ And in concluding that part of

22   the inquest, I would, at this point --

23   MR. ██████ Dr. ██████, before you would

24   conclude, I would just ask a couple follow-up questions

25   for purposes of clarity of the record.

27

1   referenced in the conference room here at the Ramsey

2   County Medical Examiner's Office, I will conclude this

3   evidentiary portions of this coroner's inquest. The

4   matter will now be in the hands of the presiding officers,

5   who will maintain custody of the various exhibits.

6   I also have provided them here today a copy

7   of the condensed -- I forget exactly what it's called, I

8   think it's called a condensed transcript. I have

9   maintained the original long-form transcripts within my

10   file, and I would stand ready to assist you in whatever

11   way you may need further; but it's my understanding you

12   will go back, conclude whatever further deliberation you

13   need, and forward a report to my office.

14   DR. ███████ That's correct, and I'll make

15   the statement that we will attempt to do this within

16   approximately the next six weeks, because we do have

17   evidence to rereview and to consider it in its totality,

18   and at that point we will issue a report drawing a

19   conclusion and would ask you to expect that sometime in

20   the next six weeks or so.

21   MR. ██████ At this point, we will conclude

22   today and can go off the record.

23   (Proceedings concluded at 10:20 a.m.)

24

25

SHADDIX & ASSOCIATES ████████

28

```
 1  STATE OF MINNESOTA)
                     ) ss.
 2  COUNTY OF DAKOTA  )

 3

 4

 5                    REPORTER'S CERTIFICATE

 6

 7         I, Colleen M. Sichko, do hereby certify that

 8  the above and foregoing transcript, consisting of the preceding

 9  27 pages is a correct transcript of my stenograph notes, and is

10  a full, true and complete transcript of the proceedings to the

11  best of my ability.

12                Dated July 31st, 2001.

13

14                _____
                  COLLEEN M. SICHKO
15                Registered Professional Reporter

16

17

18

19

20

21

22

23

24

25
```

May 2,, 2016

▮▮▮▮▮▮▮ County Attorney

▮▮▮▮▮▮▮▮▮▮▮▮▮▮▮▮▮▮▮▮

▮▮▮▮▮▮▮▮▮▮▮

RE: Pearl ▮▮▮▮▮▮, File No. ▮▮▮▮▮▮

Dear ▮▮▮▮▮▮,

Recently I picked up some records from ▮▮▮▮▮▮ County Court Administration.

They were unable to find the photographs taken in the above case. Deputy ▮▮▮▮

photographed the scene with a video camera and took still photographs. ▮▮▮▮▮▮▮▮

took photographs of the body prior to it being moved.

Could you please look into this matter and assist me in viewing the photographs.

I realize there would be a fee if I were to obtain copies. Thank you in advance.

Sincerely yours,

▮▮▮▮▮▮▮

attm: Your letter to me regarding this matter.

1

June 6, 2016

RE: Pearl

Attorney Judicial Center

Dear

Thank you for taking time out of your busy schedule on June 2, 2016 to meet with me. I would like to obtain copies of some of the pictures. There were 57 pictures taken and I only saw a few of them. I would like to make an appointment to come back and view the remaining pictures at a time that is convenient for you. Would you please have your secretary call me to set up an appointment. Thank you.

Sincerely,

1

June 6, 2016

RE: Pearl ███████████

Chief Ramsey County Medical Examiner

300 East University Avenue

Saint Paul, Minnesota 55101

Dear ███████

Last week I met with ███████, ███████ County Attorney. I viewed some of the

pictures taken in the investigation of Pearl ███████. I also had picked up the

Coroner's Inquest record that was taken in your office.

I am the witness in this case and I was not present at your questioning in the Inquest. I

have several unanswered questions that I believe you could help me to understand.

Would it be possible to arrange a meeting with you at your convenience. I can be

reached by phone or by my address. Thank you.

Sincerely,

1

July 11, 2016

RE: Pearl ███████████

Chief Ramsey County Medical Examiner

300 East University Avenue

Saint Paul, Minnesota 55101

Dear ██████████,

Thank you for taking the time to call me about the Pearl ██████████ case. The day after we talked, ██████████ left me a message on my phone that he could not meet with me, but he would scan the photos and send them to me. He did and I received the photos last week. When I was in his office in June, I showed him 4 pages of unanswered questions. I have now sent him a copy of those and have included a copy for you. These questions were formulated after searching all the records in this case. Missing are records of my lengthy testimony on this case.

The record of the Inquest with you, states all of the photos were not available at that time. The blood staining on the neck is clear. I think it would be important for you to look at the photos and see if there is a possibility that they are bruise marks.

Sincerely,

██████████

Attachment: Copy of unanswered questions.

cc: ██████████

2

July 11, 2016

Re: Pearl ████████████

Dear ████████████

Received the photos you sent me and I thank you very much. I also had sent a letter to Dr. ██████, the one who did the autopsy on Pearl ████████ He called me the day before I received your message of intent to mail the photos. We had a lengthy conversation and I informed him of my position on this case and certain facts that were included in the 27 page Inquest. He told me he would need an order from you or the police department for him to look at this case. Would you please request that Dr. ██████ take a second look at this case? As you recall, I was subpoened for the Inquest and I have not seen a copy of my lengthy testimony. Would you please send me a copy of my testimony?

Thank you for your assistance and time looking into this matter.

Sincerely,

████████████

Attachment: Copy of unanswered question

CC: ██████████ and copy of unanswered questons.

1

1. ███████████ Sheriff's Department at 0852 on 1 2/22/93 , received a 911 call from ███████ ███████ the Schwann's driver. He stated he stopped at the Pearl ███████ residence and opened the door and the house was full of smoke.

Q. Why would Pearl leave her door open?

Q. Who had damaged the door to gain entry into the home?

Deputy ███████ stated in his report that the first fireman on the scene damaged the door to gain entry.

Q. Why does he say this? Why would the fireman damage a door that was open?

Q. Why didn't he look into this? Did intruders damage that door?

2. Neighbor drove by around midnight on her way home from working at the hospital, she saw a flicker of light in the window of the house, which was unusual, as Pearl was in bed. The neighbor told ███████ months later of this strange light in Pearl's dark house.

Q. Was the flicker of light a match stick?

Q. Why did ███████ omit this in his report?

A. Spent match stick was found in house and 10 boxes of matches were removed as evidence . (in his report).

Q. Why were there 10 match boxes in the house, and why did he consider them evidence? What did he do with them?

3. A neighbor (witness) while out checking her 2 horses in a pen behind Pearl's house, heard arguing and then looked at Pearl's house, and saw 2 men come out of the house just before an explosion that lit up the area. She could clearly see the two men and heard one intruder say, " this isn't ███ house, you didn't have to do it, she is only an old woman." She gave this information during her participation in the inquest.

Q. Why was this information ignored?

Q. Why was she unable to show Dr. ███████ and Dr. ███████ where she actually was to hear and witness the men?

Q. Why did they think she needed x-ray vision, binoculars or high step ladder?

Q. Why did they continue to question her about her view from her house with sarcasm and a mocking tone?

1

Q. Why did noone walk to the location of the horse pen?

4. At ▓▓▓▓▓▓ request the neighbor collected her work schedules and called ▓▓▓▓up and informed him that Pearl died at 0015 on December 22, 1993.

Q. Why did ▓▓▓▓ omit this vital information from his report?

5. Pearl's personal documents were found at the scene carefully collected, placed in a garbage bag and soaked with an accelerant.

Q. Who did they think poured the accelerant on the papers? Why?

Q. Samples tested positive for petroleum distilate, why did they ignore this?

During the investigation, ▓▓▓▓ found a part full can of paint thinner in the basement, he seems to assume this was the accelerant.

Q. Did he know that Pearl could not use those stairs because of knee problems?

6. First fire man on the scene walked in and around the body and picked up a pillow/cushion from one of the chairs in the kitchen and tossed it outside.

Q. Why wasn't this pillow/cushion examined?

Q. Maybe would match the fibers found in the throat of the victim?

Q. Could this have been the murder weapon?

Q. What happened to this pillow?

Q. Why was only one pillow from the kitchen chairs smouldering ?

7. Dr. ▓▓▓▓, coroner, that did the autopsy, noticed scuff marks in the soot in a photo, so he assumed the victim was alive after the fire.

Q. Was he informed that the fireman walked around the victim twice?

8. The first fireman on the scene was not informed or subpeoned for a coroner's inquest.

He repeatedly told the fire marshall that something " happened here".

Q. Why did they not want him to testify?

9. Deputy ▓▓▓▓ has in his report that the fireman damaged the door to gain entry.

Q. Did they not want the fireman to testify that the door was open?

2

10. Fabric softener pad on door knob.

    Q. Who put it there, and why?

    Q. Could that had been a way to prevent finger prints?

11. All samples taken from the victim and floor around her, came back with petroleum distillate; no grease found.

    Q. Why do the reports assume that the cause of death was the upright can of grease on the stove?

12. The window was opened a crack before the fire and it was 20 degrees below zero. Pearl would not do this.

    Q. Why? Who opened the window?

13. Key witness was never questioned on motive or intruders.

    Q. Why not investigate all the facts?

14. Sheriff never went door to door to ask questions.

    Q. Isn't that important? Isn't that first line of an investigation?

15. Sheriff ███████ was informed that ██████ had all the records.

    Q Why did he refuse to talk to her`?

16. Fire Marshall and the Deputy ██████ disagree on the path of the fire.

    Q. Discrepancy should it have been questioned?

17. A witness provided information on the motivation for Pearl's death, the men who were seen were looking for incriminating records. They were at the wrong house. Deputy was informed that they came for the records.

    Q. Why didn't he ask to see the records?

    Q. Why didn't they interview the men?

18. Fire Marshall stated Pearl had been in bed and that is collaborated by the neighbor's drive by and seeing a dark house.

    Q. Intruders woke her up? Who were they?

3

19. Pearl baked earlier in the evening and left goods on the stove.

    Q. Was the stove turned on to ignite the petroleum distilate?

20. Dr. ██████ questions in the inquest was done to lead the witness to agree to his interpretation.

    Q. Why were not all parties invited?

    Q. Why not look at all the possibilities?

    Q. Why not investgate this death as a possible murder?

21. Petechial hemorrhages in the scelera of the eyes is usually due to suffocation or strangulation.

    Q. Why wasn't this considered as a cause of death?

22. Blood staining on the neck.

    Q Could she have been held down to suffocate her using the pillow?

23. ██████████ noted blood splatter on counter top and under the lip of the counter top.

    Q. Why is there blood? Was there a blow to the head?

    Q. Why wasn't she included to participate in the inquest?

██████ also noted a grease type splatter on the two cupboard doors directly above victim.

    Q. Why wasn't this grease sent to the lab for analysis?

24. Blisters and redness on the palms of her hands.

    Q. Could she have struggled to get up off the floor?

25. Death certificate changed after the inquest to read probable fatal cardiac arrhythmia

    Q. Why was this done?

26. Deputy ██████████ informed ██████████ the Fire Marshall, that Pearl died of a heart attack. There is no documentation by Dr. ██████ that Pearl had a myocardial infarction.

    Q Is that why the case was not investigated as a homicide?

    Q. Is this why all investigation seemed to end?

4